Domains is published bi-annually in the United States by South Focus Press (244 Fifth Avenue, Suite 2802, New York, New York 10001, www.southfocuspress.org) under the editorial direction of Pradeep Jeganathan at the International Centre for Ethnic Studies, Colombo, Sri Lanka.

Domains gratefully acknowledges the assistance of Trinh Nguyen and Kanchana Banerjee in the production of this issue.

Domains is a refereed journal.

Domains Two and other subsequent issues are available as books (ISBN: 097488393X, for this issue) through out the world, distributed by Ingram Book Company and Baker & Taylor in the US, Whitakers in the UK, and Ingram International in the rest of the world. These issues may be ordered from any bookstore in those countries, and is also available from amazon.com.

Domains is also available as a serial (ISSN: 1391-9768) through out the world. Subscribers in the United States, United Kingdom and Europe may purchase yearly subscriptions from www.southfocuspress.org: Institutions US$ 85.00, individuals: US$ 35.00. Subscriptions for readers in Sri Lanka are SL Rs. 750, and for South Asia and the global South are US$ 15.00 and may be ordered from The Senior Librarian, *Domains* Subscriptions, International Centre for Ethnic Studies, 2 Kynsey Terrace, Colombo 00800, Sri Lanka.

Domains welcomes submissions of between 7,500-10,000 words, from all disciplines of the social sciences and humanities, pertaining to any geographical area of the world. Both purely theoretical and empirically rich articles are valued, if original and rigorously argued; thematically important are problems of subordinate and dominant nationalisms in post-colonial spaces, questions of statehood, rule and governance, conflict resolution and constitutional reform on the one hand and gendered violence and social suffering, cultural diversity and communal co-existence on the other. *Domains* is particularly interested in post-disciplinary intellectual projects such as postcolonial feminism, critical legal studies and subaltern studies. Submissions, which should include an abstract of 150-300 words, should be sent as a MS-Word attachment to submissions@icesdomains.org. For the most current information about special issues and themes visit www.icesdomains.org.

Domains is printed on acid free paper.

For Stephen Lissenburgh
Friend & Colleague

30th April 1964 — 26th December 2004

DOMAINS

Editor
Pradeep Jeganathan
International Centre for Ethnic Studies

DOMAINS TWO

August 2005

Selvi's Revenge[1]

Mangalika de Silva.

> The struggle for existence is asserted rather than proved. It takes place but it is the exception…where there is struggle, there is struggle for power.
> — *Nietzsche*

> The resistance of others is the condition of our own development [progr`es]
> — *Michel de Certeau*

ABSTRACT

This paper narrativises two critical moments of struggle in the lives of Selvi and Pavalamma. As women, they embody the "edge of marginality" in the life of the Tamil nation. As Tamil, they rebuff the seductive nationalist claims of "community" and historical "sharedness" by pointing to the heterogeneity and multidimensionality of Tamilness. They set themselves apart from the true definition of the nation. Their transgressive defiance constitutes a riposte to delusions of nationalist "unity." It incites conditions of possibility that are enabling and constraining. Selvi and Pavalamma, in complex ways, refuse to be "nurturers" in the home of Tamil Eelam. Nationalism invokes history to "blackmail" women's Tamilness by insisting on their social and cul-

---

[1] My sincere gratitude to Qadri Ismail for support and inspiration in writing this paper. It is culled from my M.A Dissertation "Body, Agency and Sexuality of Terror in Tamil Nationalism," 1997/98, Institute of Social Studies, The Hague. I wish to thank my two supervisors Saskia Wieringa and Lily Ling as well as Jan Nederveen Pieterse, Malathi de Alwis, Jan Breman and Peter van de Veer for engaging conversations at different moments of writing this paper. The incisive comments of the two anonymous reviewers were useful in sharpening my arguments. This paper would not have been *this* paper without their suggested revisions. I am grateful to Nimanthi Rajasingham for encouraging me to submit this paper to *Domains*, to R. Cheran for facilitating my fieldwork in Toronto, the epicenter of Tamil Diaspora, in the winter of 1995 and to Kanchana Bannerjee for sensitively editing this text. Earlier versions of this paper were read at the conference on Nationalism, Identity and Minority Rights held at the Bristol University, England in August 1999, at the Amsterdam School for Social Science Research (ASSR), University of Amsterdam, The Netherlands in Fall 2000, as part of the Staff Seminar Series and subsequently at the colloquium on Women's Histories at Sarah Lawrence College, New York, in February 2001. I am grateful to all those who commented.

tural embodiment. Their stories powerfully illustrate how their self-reflexive choice of subversive Tamilness in the terrain of hegemonic nationalism is fraught with dire consequences. I have tried to capture the trajectory of this "backlash" produced by the nationalist "black-mail" by way of Selvi's revenge and Pavalamma's subversive maternity. By positing their "marginal," "intimate" story against the "grand epic" of Sacrifice, Heroism and Violence, Selvi and Pavalamma produce their own searching, sombre, subversive critique from within and from below. A subalternist critique of nationalism, as ideology, history and practice. In doing so, they imbue their sense of self with a tragic dignity. Both women view history subversively contesting the very meaning of the Political in the constitution of the nation. These fragments of experience as events of "small significance" offer a critical notion of the historical, a subversive conception of the political. This paper, then, is in defence of the "marginal" story. Finally, while their stories force into stark narrative visibility the historiographical contest, they simultaneously force us to think anew the troubled nexus of women and the nation.

This paper looks at two moments of violence in the history of the Tamil nation. Selvi and Pavalamma belong irreducibly to their time, a time of grief, suffering and destruction. Both women are betrayers of the Tamil nation, revolting against the tyranny of history. My focus is primarily on Selvi, a child recruit abducted by the LTTE (The Liberation Tigers of Tamil Eelam) at a tender age of ten to serve the interests of Tamil nationalism and re-abducted by the Sinhala state to serve the interests of Sinhala nationalism. Selvi gets accustomed to life as an orphan in the tumult of Tamil nationalism. The political turmoil in the region engulfs her when her foster brother, Sritharan, goes missing. Villainised by the LTTE for his proximity with the Sinhala army, Sritharan is put to death by the LTTE for "betraying" the Tamil cause. His murder becomes Selvi's personal tragedy, a tragedy that strikes cruelly in the turbulence of her childhood. For Selvi, the perpetrators were oppressive men undaunted by the Andersonian angst; the will to kill and die for the nation. As a child, not quite conscious of a primordial Tamilness, she becomes the object of Tamil nationalism's lust for hegemony. She gets constituted as a subject in the process of her politicisation, aimed at accentuating her consciousness as a Tamil. The sole purpose of her Tamilness, in the dominant logic of nationalism, must be to nourish and defend the mother terrain, the territory of Tamil Eelam and grow up in the bosom of the Tamil nation. Tamil nationalism mercilessly wounds Selvi to remind her of her own Tamilness, her loyalty to the Tamil nation and the dire repercussions that would follow any sign of shift of loyalty by snuffing out her brother's life. The grief caused by his unjust murder transforms her consciousness, leading to a crisis that is ultimately resolved by returning the revenge on her oppressors – the Tamil nation.

Pavalamma, the "criminalised" Tamil mother, is imprisoned in the nation of Tamil Eelam. Her crime, a consequence of her own burden, a social burden imposed on women like her by the Tamil patriarchy, is the burden of motherhood. As a Tamil mother, her Tamilness and maternity must be in the interest of nationalism, a demand made by the Tamil community, a condition necessary to advance the cause of the nation. Whether women desire the nation or not, they are caught in the ruse of power so that their desire is not so much repressed as coded. Pavalamma's Tamilness is seen in opposition to the demands of hegemonic Tamil nationalism. Her sons are engaged in a politics of resistance, aimed at challenging the dominance of the LTTE in the field of Tamil politics. Pavalamma, the "renegade" mother, the Tamil nation's Other, is made to pay a heavy price for her sons' belligerence. Tiger women, her own perpetrators of violence, physically mutilate her body as a form of punishment for her "misplaced," "misguided," "subversive," Tamilness and maternity.

But why focus on these two specific historical moments of violence? For both Selvi and Pavalamma, as history shadows and constrains, incites and thwarts, it also returns with a vengeance. Their space, a non place, a zone of non being. Constrained by the region's past, with no real break from the burden of history, they struggle to step outside the nation to interrogate its politics of Othering. Their experience is a rude reminder that nation has been historically forged, constituted in opposition to the Other. The two moments of violence make visible the tensions at play between the two processes of signification and politicisation. The nation of Tamil Eelam invokes history to blackmail women's Tamilness by coercively insisting on a notion of a national Tamil unity, a Tamil nationalist essence. By contrast, both Selvi and Pavalamma invoke familial bonds, emotional bonds that are meaningful to them, ties that are indefensible to Tamil Eelam. Both women embody a difference, a Tamilness that dissents, opposes, critiques, subverts, a subversive Tamilness anathematised by hegemonic nationalism represented by the LTTE. Difference, in the form of female subversion, has no dwelling in the home of Tamil Eelam. Indeed, nationalism cannot be at home with difference. Any sign of oppositional Tamilness is seen as threatening to the larger Tamil community it imagines. The moments of violence, lived yet suppressed, in the lives of Selvi and Pavalamma, bring into narrative visibility, registers of the everyday; contingent, particular struggles, a prosaic of resistance. The moments of violence constitute a complex conjuncture/disjuncture that produces the condition of possibility of critique, a subalternist critique that challenges power. It questions the imperia of legitimacy, the very legitimacy of nationalism; its uniformising influence, its ersatz aura of sacrifice, violence and heroism.

What the two fragments attempt to map is the experience of the edge, living at the very limits of life, at the extreme, at the borderline of possibilities. This I urge is the critical import of the fragment, that it resists the singularisation of the political, the singularisation of the nationalist imagination and struggles for a different imagining. In his account of the Hindu Muslim riots in India, Gyanendra Pandey writes; 'part of the "fragmentary" point of view lies in this, that it resists the drive for a shallow homogenisation and struggles for other, potentially richer definitions of the "nation" and the future political community.'[2] But the point is that the very struggle to define the nation itself involves a contestation of history, a historiographical contest. The discursive challenge is not to insist on richer definitions of the nation, though who defines the nation is a question of power. But more critically to underscore the point that nation's history has no place for other memories or histories, memories of those pushed to the extreme of marginality. As the struggles of Selvi and Pavalamma well illustrate, nation is a lived reality for women. They refuse to fantasise about a future political community while

---

[2] Gyanendra Pandey, "In Defence of the Fragment: Writing about Hindu Muslim Riots in India Today." *Economic and Political Weekly*, Vol. XXVI. No. 11 & 12. (March 1991), 559.

insisting that if any future political community is to be imagined, it has to be located in the disjunctured present.

And why reclaim these fragments for history? Ranajith Guha suggests we dignify them as textual sites. To cite from Guha; 'To read these statements, as an archive, is to dignify them as the textual site for a struggle to reclaim for history an experience buried in a forgotten crevice of our past.'[3] Guha does not extrapolate what dignify means. As sites of politicisation, experiences of Selvi and Pavalamma enable us to rethink/reimagine the political in moments of struggle so that women emerge not as a unity but as a fractured reality. Guha seems particularly unconcerned with the forms of the political in moments of violence. To historicise, I contend, is to recover the texture of struggle. To dignify is to capture the forms of the political the fragments invoke, the forms, which help produce a critique of the nation. If the writing of history is concerned with writing the personal, then the personal is a way of writing the political. The critical purchase of the fragment lies in the fact that it resists history's arrogance of definitiveness and struggles to recover a sense of the political out of shards of memory.

The incomplete story of Selvi, fore-grounded in this paper, evokes an uncompromising insistence. It contumaciously demands to be read against - alongside and in opposition to - nationalist history. It seeks, through this retelling, to avenge history. For it is in the name of history that women's body is conquered and colonised. So that history emerges as a seemingly powerful story, flaunting its excess, conceit and vanity. The postcolonial feminist text intervenes to deconstruct its shallow, seductive patriarchal promises. It calls history itself into account by interrogating the historical (masculine) claims made in the name of the political. I read Selvi's story as a metonym, a metaphor, as a signifier of a counter imaginary. It is an oppositional textual intervention to evacuate women's experiential narratives in conditions of unfreedom and to unveil the entanglement of the local with the national(ist) in intersecting, colluding fields of power. Such collusion points to the possibility of transgression, collaboration, rebellion and adversarial engagement. I prefer to use stories as a

---

[3] Ranajit Guha, "Chandra's death." *Subaltern Studies V.* (ed) R. Guha. (New Delhi: Oxford University Press, 1987), 142.

method of testing out theories inspired by feminist philosophy that knowledge is contextual, relational and situated. But what I have here is not the full story. It is a fragment exhibiting the 'recalcitrantly ambiguous character of lived experience.' I read her story as an experiment in micro history. It is an experiential notion of micro history. This paper is in defence of the fragment.

I want to begin by contending how both the nationalist projects, Sinhala and Tamil, given their incommensurability and dissonance, converge, collide, negotiate and overlap to produce the material/ideological conditions of the possibility of violence to perpetuate a culture of control/containment and consolidate their power.

This paper, then, is a subalternist critique of nationalism, as ideology, practice and history.[4] As repositories of tradition and signifiers of community identity, women's body constitutes the terrain where the contest over "nation" takes place. Selvi's revenge questions the ideological basis of the singularity of nationalist historical narrative by inserting the heterogeneity and plurality of social and cultural embodiment. It does so in ways that make visible processes of knowledge production and meaning constructions that counter the authority of the nation's violent epistemology. When identities are in crisis, when cultures are in conflict, the female body demarcates the sexual, racial and national boundaries of the struggle. Body is a site of power for production, violence and conquest. The locus of cultural investment is in the sexual body, which is also the national body. This is shifted to a Foucauldian register of the cultural body, the register of the useful body, the productive body. Selvi's body is made productive to nationalism as she morphs into a fighting Tiger cadre, at a critical juncture in the struggle for Eelam. The body is hence under a continuous process of subjectivation. As a historical moment in the praxis of transgressive politics, her story as text, implicates history's exclusion of her own past in a genealogy of violence of the nation. Such exclusions, her text asserts, are ultimately epistemological and political.

There are various sites (field), sights (artefact or object), stages and templates upon which history is constructed as a cultural

---

[4] The idea is Ismail's.

object. The narratives of Selvi and Pavalamma interrupt and disrupt the linear representation of history as "grand" event. They decentre and deconstruct the dominant nationalist narrative which privileges the "nation" as a "horizontal comradeship" (of male nationals) unified by a "common remembering" and "shared" past. They displace the "heroic, celebratory and elaborate" idiom of nationalist narrative that glorifies the "unity" and "purity" of the struggle by opening up a discursive space to speak of smaller narratives, intimate stories and events of "small significance."

This essay then begins with a transgression.[5] The event is recounted by a woman, Selvi, who re-lives the experience of pain of war, seared in her memory, revisiting its multi-dimensionality, its hold on the present and the nervously anticipated uncertain future. The authority of the law had appropriated her experience discursively inscribing it as an act of criminality, treachery, a terrorist act undermining the supreme authority of that final arbiter, the State. The discursive appropriation of the event by that most authoritative of ideological apparatuses, the law achieves a function that serves the purpose of denying it legitimacy, representation, voice and meaning. It is necessary to historicise an event precisely for this reason, as a frequent occurrence in a society ravaged by decades of ethnic conflict where such events are celebrated in the valorisation of "nation" and community persuaded to remember them as "excesses" or "reprisals" only in order for them to recede in human memory as mere "errors." It is not merely the will of the law as the primary interpreter of the State's authority that interposes its own purpose on the event inextricably intertwined with Selvi's life. Her continued incarceration and the indefinite detention under repressive PTA and ER[6] suggest the carceral complicity of Sinhala and Tamil nationalisms. Instituted under the guise of curbing "terrorist" activities, these capricious laws are designed to drastically curtail fundamental freedoms of ordinary

---

[5] For this and several other illuminating insights, I am indebted to Guha, *op. cit.*, 1987.

[6] Prevention of Terrorism Act & Emergency Regulations. PTA was enacted in 1979 under the First Executive system introduced in 1978. ERs were first imposed in the whole island in 1971 to quell the first southern insurgency led by the Janatha Vimukthi Peramuna (JVP) People's Revolutionary Front.

Tamil people. In the dominant nationalist narrative, Selvi's past[7] is sanctioned, condemned for obscurity. Since the event unfolds within the material and discursive domain of Tamil nationalism, which claims to represent the will of the larger Tamil community in its violent opposition to Sinhala hegemony, it assumes greater salience in the way the story of Tamil nationalism is written. In its heroic, celebratory and elaborate idiom, the story of Tamil nationalism is a story (event) of an oppressed community (minority)[8] resisting the Sinhala community's (majority) enforcement of subjugation and repression, unified by a common "remembering" and a "shared" past. Marginal and marginalised in these edifying nationalist accounts are "events of small significance" that are intricately woven out of the nationalist narrative. Often, glorifying the unity, a shared past and the morality of the struggle serve the purpose of sacralising violent crimes of extreme nature committed by those waging the struggle, enabling the "authentic popular protest" (event) to return to the public nationalist imagination. Within the story of "nation," Selvi's story, as a narrative of "small events," represents a specific historically contingent moment of the struggle where the effect of this distinction is amplified. If what is deemed "profane" gets excluded and thereby erased from the collective memory[9] of nationalist struggle, such exclusions pro-

---

[7] Hall's definition of subjectivity is constitutive of a narrative, story and history. Quoted in Parry. B. "Resistance theory, theorising resistance or two cheers for nativism" in *Colonial Discourse/Post Colonial Theory*, eds., Francis Baker, Peter Hulme & Margaret Iversen. (Manchester University Press 1994), 175.

[8] While acknowledging this formulation's hegemony in the linguistic order of English language, minority/majority binarism, in the vernacular translations, intensifies the axis of power/knowledge, positing the minor as the derogatory other of the privileged major. It is important to note that these are not natural entities but constructions that simultaneously hierarchise and subordinate. In a given semantic and disciplinary field, they acquire majority/minority status. The point is certain histories become historically dominant by logic of difference, which marks 'minority' histories as non-historical, making them historically unutterable.

[9] The "reliability" of personal narratives as a historical document has been subjected to much inquiry by James. F Young and others. Its "ephemeral" nature, distance from facts, flexible character and its propensity to misrepresentation have been problematised by ethnographers and historians. The commonly acknowledged fact is its little validity in representing group or collective experience. Moss argues how 'recollection itself is a complex piece of evidence' constituting three key elements: event or reality; the memory of it the testimony which becomes an interpretive act. 'Memory, he says, is tricky with respect to reality.' Yet the fact that recollections provoke understanding and insight cannot simply be disputed. For James Young, oral history is a matter of

voke interrogation of narrative strategies by which a people gets constructed into a "nation." This paper is an attempt not to speculate on "small events" but to uncover and narrativise repressed histories buried in the "ethnic" rubble. It is in the interest of nationalism that such events are ghettoised, forgotten and effaced by the force of its own will. In retelling of the extraordinary event where the ordinary woman's will to resist comes into conflict with the "nation's" will to enforce, both the judicial and nationalist discourses as authorised accounts are implicated in reducing the physical occurrence of the event to mere criminality glossing over the context, structure and process that conditioned and shaped the event. The very fact that the event occurred in whatever unspecified ways justifies a textual intervention[10] that revisits the material with the purpose of reclaiming the event for a critical history of the present. The precariously complex event, as it is re-narrated, bears Selvi subalternised within the subaltern narrative, as the only witness to a series of violent acts that occurred in history. Acts that are a direct outcome of a clash of wills, struggles over meaning that menacingly point to a convergence in the mode of resistance between the dominant and the subaltern forms of rebellion. At the murky interface lies agency bounded by the prevailing ideology and hegemony, the hegemony of Tamil nationalism. Selvi's story lies in its entanglement of the local with the national, be it Sinhala or Tamil nationalism – as ideology, practice and as history. The story begins with Selvi, a member of the Tamil community, from the margins of the Tamil community, at the horizon of its contested history. Yet she is not beyond the pale. The story must begin with her because as a subject, she is still the site of contest over "nation." As a marginal story, it functions to cast doubt on the major, to suspect and question the historically grand claims of the major, to argue tenaciously how certain events/pasts are edged out or peripheralised, silenced, deauthorised, made subordinate in the dominant moment of

---

memory, reconstruction and imagination. Unlike written history that tends to hide lines of construction, oral testimonies retain the process of construction, the activity of witness. In Ritu Menon & Kamla Bhasin, eds., *Borders and Boundaries: Women in India's Partition* (New Jersey: Rutgers University Press, 1999), 28-29. The writing of history, I argue, is a social practice involving processes of recovery, discovery, construction, deconstruction and reconstruction.
[10] Ranajit Guha, *op. cit.*, 1987, 135.

narrative logic and historicisation and to ground the struggle for freedom in the lives of subaltern histories. Rescuing such "treacherous" pasts is ultimately linked to democratic struggles, a struggle against dominance and a necessary condition for the ontology of the subject, in making possible and visible a counter imaginary, an oppositional philosophy and an emancipatory politics. Selvi's story (text) then is an "accomplice"[11] in the constitution of a critique of historicity contingently opening up possibilities for a critical history of the present.

I met Selvi in early 1996. She was locked up in a clandestine detention cell along with many others, away from public scrutiny. She was the youngest in a group of mostly adult Tamil women, detained under various charges. The public was largely unaware of a detention cell, housed inside a Buddhist temple, located in the outskirts of Colombo. I managed to spend a few hours with the women while observing the conditions inside the cell and listening to their tales of horror. Selvi, I noticed, was most eager to make an impression and insisted on speaking to me. My ears turned to her and the fragment that appears below was all I could smuggle out of the cell. Selvi recollects:

> My brother, Sritharan, used to hawk vegetables in the market in Kalmunai[12] town. The place was under heavy army control. They used to buy their daily supplies from him. He would send rations regularly to the soldiers in the camp. It was his sole means of livelihood. The LTTE[13] came to know and they were not happy. They started intimidating him, threatening him with death if he did not heed their warning. He continued regardless. A few days later, he disappeared. The day following his disappearance, four armed militant men came to our house. Later I discovered they were LTTE men. My father and brother were both at sea. There was no one around in the vicinity. I was alone. They blind-

---

[11] Qadri Ismail, "Discipline and colony: The English Patient and the crow's nest of post coloniality" in *Postcolonial Studies: Culture, Politics, Economy*, (1999) 2 (3), 403-436.

[12] Situated on the Batticaloa-Karaithivu road in the eastern province, presently the main theatre of war, a region severely affected by the ethnic violence.

[13] The Liberation Tigers of Tamil Eelam are fighting a separatist war with the Sri Lankan state since 1979.

folded me and hurled me up into a van. One of them said that I could see my brother that they were taking me there, to their camp that he was in one of their camps…(my italics)

I was only ten years old when they abducted me. When we reached the camp, I heard my brother's screaming voice. It became louder and I realised he was screaming in pain. When I finally saw him, he was hung suspended on the branch of a tree, arms and legs tied with a rope and blindfolded. He was severely beaten. I saw his blood splattered body. He had wounds on his arms, chest and legs. Blood was spouting out. He was writhing in pain…unable to speak… They had been torturing him since the day he was taken. They said they punished him for disobeying their orders…He was asked to join the movement. He refused…he was a traitor, he betrayed the struggle, he betrayed Tamils by collaborating with the army, the Sinhala army, he must be punished…

I cried…they asked me if I would join them…I did not say anything…They began to terrorise me and yet, the image of the mutilated body of my brother was such a gruesome sight…I was helpless…all I could do was weep…I remember how they continued beating him laughing loud, insulting him, abusing him…they repeated their threats to kill me if I refused to join while beating him…few moments later, he was dead…they shot him. They threatened to kill my father and brother if I disagreed. I was afraid of losing them, I agreed…

I was given military training for one year. After my training, they decided to send me off to Jaffna. Ajitha became my best friend during the months I spent in the camp. She persuaded me not to go to Jaffna. I was having a chest pain and was afraid to go there by ferry. Six months later, I escaped from the women's camp in Karaithivu, Batticaloa…She knew I was angry and bitter about what they did to my brother. I confided in her. I disclosed my intention of revenge to Ajitha. She was cautious but supportive. Together we devised a plan to kill him, he was the real enemy, he killed my brother. The day before the plan was carried out, Ajitha did not report to work. That afternoon, a banner was put up for her. The Tigers announced that she died in combat…

The men had been observing us. The two camps were adjacent to each other. We could see them from the sentry. They could watch us. We could watch them. The same group of men who killed my brother had questioned Ajitha. They were suspicious. She had been interrogated that morning to extract the 'secret' of our intimacy. Ajitha had confessed fearing for her life. She told them of the plan to revenge...they killed her...

That afternoon, I was on duty.[14] I saw him approach me. He was so near...I pulled my gun and fired...he was lying on the ground. I ran into the nearby hut, dropped the gun, I was in uniform. I had kept my clothes there. I quickly changed and ran as fast as I could, trekking through the shrubs and came back home. My father had vacated the house and left the village. They had moved to Batticaloa. I had no place to go. My father's neighbour, an old man, was very kind to me. I stayed with him. My father would hire his boat occasionally to go to sea...

Few weeks passed. A member of TELO[15] used to visit this house. First, I did not know he was a TELO cadre. He seemed interested and asked if I would marry him. My neighbour uncle rejected his proposal. He left...One day the Sinhala army cordoned off the area for a search operation. Villagers gave information to the army that I had links with the Tigers. My uncle and I were questioned. He told them I had no connection with any militant group...

Weeks passed by. One afternoon, while I was playing with the children in the neighbourhood, two vehicles screeched to a halt in front of the verandah. They were TELO members. There were several of them. I was dragged out of the house and driven out of the village. I spent the rest of the months with a Muslim family. The TELO member who was urging me to marry him kept exerting pressure...I resisted...A few months later, my reactions were different. The woman in the house gave me some charmed milk to drink[16]...My attitude softened...I started liking him...we lived together. I gave birth to a son. We continued to live in

---

[14] For Selvi, duty served two objectives. Obligation (familial/familiar) to avenge the death of her brother was one awaiting her. She was serving the killers ("nation"/unknown/strange) in order to perform this purifying act.

[15] Tamil Eelam Liberation Organisation, a rival paramilitary group fighting the LTTE.

[16] Milk, a protean fluid, is symbolic of valour. The idea of Tamil mother feeding their sons with heroic milk is still dominant. There are references to heroic milk in classical Tamil literature. See C. S. Lakshmi, "Mother, mother community and mother politics in Tamil Nadu," in *Economic and Political Weekly*, (Oct/20-29, 1990). Obeyesekere contends that milk is an image of love and nurture. Bitter milk, according to him, is used as a symbol of punishment for betrayal of loved ones. It is associated with negation. (*Medusa's Hair: An Essay on Personal Symbols and Religious Experience*. (Chicago: University of Chicago Press, 1981). However, it is not clear what the milk given to Selvi, contained.

the same house. Three years later, the Sinhala army came in search of him. They wanted him to work for them, provide information about LTTE activity. First he refused to go. The child was only three years. We wanted to give him the father's name. We consulted an astrologer for the naming ceremony.[17] The name had to be changed. He looked so much like the father. His birth would cause him harm, the astrologer said.

The pressure on him to work with the army was mounting. He finally relented...A few days later he was killed. The body was returned to me. Meanwhile, my father came looking for me. My uncle had informed him of my whereabouts. We returned home with my child. The LTTE was everywhere. I did not want to stay any longer. The situation was very unsafe for me. I gave the child to my aunt (father's sister) and returned to live with the Muslim family. During the months that followed, I worked as a domestic. My father knew the landlord. I worked for three months but was never happy there...I yearned to leave the village, so I came to the station where I met Janaki who was then employed in Colombo. I decided to go with her and look for a job. On our way in Polannaruwa, we were arrested (abducted?). I had no identification. Five or six policemen questioned all of us. They said they would assault anyone who refused to give information. That we would be forced to sit on soda bottles if we did not tell them the "truth." They asked me if I served the movement, took part in military operations, made bombs, killed soldiers. I was terrified and feared being tortured. I told them everything that had happened. They recorded my statement. I could not read it. I did not read it. I did not understand the language. I was asked to sign the paper. I was later told that it was a document authorising indefinite detention. I was transferred to a police cell in Kotahena and from there to Gangodawila.

I did not take part in any attacks. My duties were mainly logistical. I would carry supplies of ammunition, T-56, bullets, automatic rifles, grenades and military fatigues. I was stationed at a sentry, which was a clandestine entry to the camp. Ajitha and I would guard bunkers. She became my best friend since we always worked together.

My desire to revenge was great. From the day my brother was killed, I was waiting for the moment of my own

---

[17] A customary practice in traditional Sri Lankan society. In Tamil tradition, there have been two major customs; One: naming son/daughter after grandparents. The other is to name son/daughter after family god/goddess. Personal communication with R. Cheran, on 20/09/1998.

liberation. It was a duty towards my brother. It had to be done. He took my brother's life. He had no right to live. Revenge was more than what I could ask for. I valued his life more than I cared for mine. I wasn't afraid of death...I had to sacrifice my life for the sake of my brother...I could not be in peace...I loved him...he took care of me...he would buy me clothes...I respected him...I had to honour him...

I was an orphan. I never saw my own father. Both of my parents were from Kalmunai. It was a mixed marriage. He left my mother when she was in hospital for delivery. I was an only child. She committed suicide soon after my birth. My foster father had adopted me. He had a big family. He had fifteen children, some adopted, some of them his own children. My foster mother died when I turned three. She decided to put an end to her miserable life. They never told me I was a foster child. I never went to school. I would often play with my brothers and sisters. I was very close to two male siblings. I loved both of them dearly...'[18]

What we have before us is, visibly, a series of fragments from the past. The shards of a dismembered past is united by a series of linkages forming a narrative which plays a role in the exchange between 'the familiar and the remarkable between the quotidian and the historic.'[19] The torn fabric of the past as a residuum constitutes an anecdote, an "untamed fragment" that speaks of a history crowded with "frantic and autonomous events." It provides authenticity - Selvi's own voice, as a witness, is a genuine testimony to the event described – and the condition of contextuality. The narrative material does not convey fully how the story begins or ends. Fragments of memory and remembrances, both bitter and tender, are strung together in a sequence that has no chronology. Yet there hovers over her telling, 'the protective shadow of a coherent narrative' exhibiting the 'recalcitrantly ambiguous character of lived experience.'[20] And for purposes of historiography, especially against the

---

[18] Selvi was emotionally close to her two elder brothers with whom she developed a deep bond.

[19] Guha, *op. cit.*, 139.

[20] Valentine Daniel, *Charred Lullabies: Chapters In An Anthropography of Violence.* (Princeton: Princeton University Press, 1997), 179.

force of the nationalist thrust[21] that conceals and obfuscates histories, that mar the "authenticity" and "purity" of the struggle, the task
of an anthropologist must be to return to the small drama, retrieve
the narrative, as part of an unfolding history, a metaphor for oppositional imagination. Selvi's narrative must be wrenched from the discursive domain since she has no authority to write about her own
history. Women like her are always written about.[22] Throughout my
inquiry, I remain conscious of my position as combing a "testimony"
for her evidence. Her story needs to be retold given the disciplinary
grid of the law finds her guilty of "crimes" against the State. In the
eyes of the law, she stands as the accused, made to confess "atrocities" perpetrated against a "sovereign" State. The State, as the supreme commander thereby, "retains" its moral high ground,
absolving itself of all responsibility for arbitrary arrest, torture during interrogation, incarceration without trial. The militant groups,
too, remain outside of this jurisdiction. For the patriarchal State,
Selvi 'served as a cadre in the Tiger movement, an act of terrorism.'
For the Tigers, she 'betrayed the separatist cause, their freedom
struggle, their realisation of the yet to be fulfilled ideal, Tamil Ee-

---

[21] Hegemonic nationalism is power embodied in the taken for granted "forms of
everyday life." Hegemony is subtle, pervasive and ultimately difficult to contest because it subsumes the forms that structure actions and beliefs. If ideology represents
the conscious, hegemony represents the unconscious. (See Diana Crane, *The Sociology of Culture.* (Oxford: Blackwell, 1994), 102.

[22] The present day nationalist violence and Tamil women's experience is an integral
part of collective Tamil experience since women and men constitute the Tamil community. No Tamil community is fully non hierarchical unless women play an important role in shaping and defining it. Selvi's experience must form part of the social
history of Tamil experience since experience is constituted through narrative. (See
Margaret R. Somers & Gloria D. Gibson, "Reclaiming the epistemological other:
narrative and the social constitution of identity, in *Social Theory and The Politics of
Identity,* Craig Calhoun (ed.) (Oxford: Blackwell, 1994)). Joan W. Scott argues that it
is not individuals who have experience but subjects who are constituted through
narrative. Hence experience is at once always already an interpretation and in need
of interpretation. (See her "Experience" in *Feminists Theorize the Political,* Judith
Butler and Joan W. Scott (ed.) (New York: Routledge, 1992). However, it seems useful to point out how certain experience of women tends to get subsumed under the
awesome weight of the social and show as Spivak suggests, different ways in which
women can make strategic use of their experience. Since knowledge of how experience is produced, interpreted, mediated and represented enables an acknowledge-
ment and transcendence of that context. See also B Skeggs' "Introduction" in
Feminist Cultural Theory: Process and Production, ed., Beverley Skeggs. (Manchester: Manchester University Press), 15-18.

lam.'[23] The forcible abduction of Sritharan, his murder at the hands of the Tigers, and Selvi's abduction and recruitment into the movement do not constitute facts. They are unrelated or irrelevant to the larger event. They nevertheless serve the interests of the two hegemonies, its use and deployment of "crime" as purposeful action. 'Murder is the point at which history intersects with crime,' according to Foucault and the site of that intersection is the 'narrative of crime.'[24] The all too common violence, trivialised and naturalised by the tolerance cultures of terror, have of cruelty and the discursive strategy of the law designed to rid Selvi's testimony of all political validation leaving the mere superficial facts of "when," "what," "how" and "where" of a "crime." The force of the law makes Selvi's abduction and forcible recruitment into a "voluntary act," designating it as a "case," turning her into a "traitor," "terrorist," and all the actants exonerated and set free. The State is impervious to its own criminality; reabduction of Selvi. She languishes imprisoned 'in the present as she narrates the past.'[25] To re-read Selvi's statement as an event therefore is not merely to dignify them as 'the textual site for a struggle to reclaim for history an experience buried in a forgotten crevice of the (nationalist) past.'[26] But more importantly, to situate the event within the life of a (Tamil) community and to acknowledge Selvi's – caught in a contest between two kinds of politics – struggle to cope, unsuccessfully and problematically though not without agency in all its complexity, with a crisis.

Colonising space

Kalmunai is located in the Ampara district on the more populous south eastern shore in the eastern province of Sri Lanka. Ethnically diverse and multi caste, the villagers mostly engage in fishing, with isolated signs of economic prosperity and some extremely poor.

---

[23] The envisaged future nation state of Tamil Eelam
[24] Michel Foucault, *I, Pierre Riviere*....cited in Guha, (1988), 139.
[25] Alan Munslow, *Deconstructing History* (London: Routledge, 1997), 129. Tied intricately to the idea of the past then is the notion of subjectivity which as Hall has suggested is at once a narrative, story and history.
[26] Guha. *op. cit.*, 142.

They are mostly Tamil speaking[27] Hindus, Muslims and a minority of Sinhalese, matrilineal and caste conscious villagers. The social organisation, with its pronounced matrilineal and matrilocal elements, has historical roots in Kerala. The Tamils and Muslims collectively share their roots, with the latter having acquired the matrilineal system through intermarriage between Muslim men and local women.[28] The majority of greater Kalmunai's community are fishermen and some are paddy farmers. Most families, even among the fishing community, do not own their ferry and some are landless.[29] A rural proletariat, they rent fishing boats to go to sea or work as day labourers in other people's fields or boats. Patriarchal domination is asserted in the complex matrix of kinship, caste, community and family relations. Sources of female power are located in traditions of self-restraint, subservience as well as transgressive practices of protest and rebellion. Images of motherhood, as a dominant cultural/nationalist trope, evoke veneration and awe. While often the community makes women a prey to male lust, they are represented as creatures of loose morals and easy virtue in dominant male literary texts.

Patriarchal laws, religion, deeply entrenched superstitions, casteism and dowry system structure women's lives. Feudal ideology blends with patriarchal morality reinforcing separate spheres for men and women. Notions of purity/impurity, good/evil, goddess/whore govern Tamil womanhood. Transgressions of social norms of femininity of achcham (fear), madam (modesty), naanam (coyness) and payirppu (charm) as the unwritten law inscribes women's subjectivity and invites strong opposition that often accompanies stigma, ostraci-

---

[27] According to the 1981 census, (the last census available) Tamils numbered about 40% of eastern provinces' one million inhabitants. Muslims comprised 32% and Sinhalese 25% of the population along with small numbers of plantation Tamils and others. See Joke Schrijvers, "Tamil-Muslim violence, gender and ethnic relations in Eastern Sri Lanka" in *Nethra*, April-June, Vol. 2, No. 3. International Centre for Ethnic Studies, (ICES) Colombo (1998), 14.

[28] Dennis McGilvray, "Households in Akkaraipattu: dowry and domestic organisation among the matrilineal Tamils and Moors of Sri Lanka" in *Society From The Inside Out: Anthropological Perspectives on The South Asian Household*, eds., John N. Gray & David J. Mearns. (London: Sage, 1989), 192-235.

[29] Mark Whitaker, "A compound of many histories: the many pasts of an east coast Tamil community" in *Sri Lanka: History and the Roots of Conflict*, ed., Jonathan Spencer (London: Routledge, 1990), 149.

sation, violent assault and even death as in katpalippu (rape). The notion of katpu is a regulatory normative ideal that separates chaste/impure women. Katpu is believed to give Tamil women sakti, their strength and power. In the notion of virginity is embodied the idea of power. Culturally, women's defiance is associated with negative femininity.

Like many other regions in the east, Kalmunai has several histories that intersect with the life of the community: mythic history, cosmic history, temple history, provincial caste history, nationalist history, colonial history, and academic history.[30] There are regional and cultural differences that divide the Tamil community of north and east based also on other power axes like caste, education and employment. Power, wealth and resources were concentrated in Jaffna, which gradually became the stronghold of militant activism leading to an armed struggle. The northern Tamils, mostly Vellala[31] caste, held their Jaffna-centric ideological sway over the east driven by other forms of historical consciousness. Nationalist history, on the east coast, had its initial roots in appeals to a common culture and Tamilness that characterised Tamil politics since the 1930s. Tamil separatist nationalism represented by a conservative, Vellala and Jaffna-oriented political groups came to be viewed with resentment and cynicism, an ideological practice that was more in the interest of Jaffna Tamils. The war radically altered such sentiments when the region's own provincial historical forms and patterns of dominance were threatened by both Sinhala and Tamil nationalism. The Sinhala state's successive attacks on villages, in militarily crushing the Tamil rebellion, led to large scale displacements of Tamils, Muslims and Sinhalese in the mid-1980s with the outbreak of Eelam war 2. The Tiger movement's genocidal campaign against minority Muslims, culminating in the forceful eviction of 500,000 Muslims from the northern peninsula in 1990, led to an erosion in ethnic relations between the two communities drawing them into the conflict. A series

---

[30] *op. cit.* 150.

[31] Jaffna's caste system is based on a hierarchy of caste comprising of Vellala (the land owning/farming), Karayars, Koviyar, Pandarams (the middle castes), The lower castes; Nalavas, Pallars, Paraiyars, Vannars (dhobi), Ambattars (barbers) and the lowest, the Thurumbars (washer men for the low caste). Personal communication with R.Cheran, 9/9/1999.

of massacres of Muslims, targeting public places of worship and sites of communal sharing exacerbated tensions, resulted in reprisals and counter attacks on Tamil areas.[32] The LTTE seized on the growing hostility and antagonism between Tamils and Muslims to strengthen their own position in the east by recruiting cadres from the region. The Sinhalese were driven out, particularly from the border areas. Decades of war and the gradual militarisation of the north and east have created multiple centres of power, with the army and the LTTE fighting for territorial dominance and control. A number of paramilitaries run their own sentries, prisons and concentration camps in the east collectively or in collusion with the military in their search for insurgents to 'discipline and punish' their common enemy.

It is against this historical dynamics of a nationalist past that Kalmunai and its community must be seen. Selvi inhabits this multi caste rural space where the borders and boundaries of the "nation" are being redefined, redemarcated and redrawn. Separatist war became the means by which the "national" came into "being-in-the-world." Previously existing social kinship ties were transformed, relocating sentiments of longing, belonging, allegiance and loyalty - that historically were nurtured in the sanctity of family - in the "sacred" space of the "Nation." Nationalism posed the question of "belonging" in a way that polarised choice and allegiance aggravating antagonisms. One gets included in the community of the "nation" by foregoing familiar signs of intimacy; family, marriage, kinship ties. Separatist war or separation assumes a dreadful meaning. It evokes a metaphor for a people violently displaced, communities divided, families torn apart, children orphaned, men killed, women widowed. For Selvi, it symbolises an irreparable loss, not merely the loss of her brother, his brutal killing authorised by the members of the "nation" embodying the new family or kin group. The killing, as an event, signals her separation from her own family where she grew up as an orphaned, adopted daughter and sister. Her childhood memories of being abandoned by her father and left <u>unprotected and unsheltered</u> by her mother and her own

---

[32] On 12th July 1990, the LTTE massacred 75 Muslims including children, women returning from Kattankudy. This was followed on 3rd August 1990 by a massacre of 122 men and boys at a prayer in two mosques at Kattankudy and on 11th August 1990. 126 Muslim children, men and women were hacked to death in several villages in Eravur. Cited in Schrijvers, 1998. 17.

by her mother and her own estrangement from her "husband" are vividly etched in her mind. Her world is familiar with signs of separation, that trope of vulnerability, savagery which marks a radical rupture in her symbolic world, loss of self and subjectivity–more importantly her desires, dreams and possibilities. She shuns the nationalist' indulgence of fantasy of a "horizontal comradeship"[33], instead affirms her identity, however problematically, as sister of her murdered brother and by affirming embraces a relationality, a sociality at once both familial and intimate. Identity is not conceived of as a boundary to be maintained but as a nexus of relations and transactions that engage her daily.[34] Her loyalty to her brother implies enslavement to familial values. Unlike the "empowered" Tiger woman for whom the Other's annihilation is contingent upon the total obscurity of the self, Selvi represents the "subjugated" woman of the patriarchal nuclear family. Unlike the Tiger women whose familial devotion is replaced by a filial devotion to a fraternal community, Selvi embraces a "sheltered" domesticity, abrogates the virtues of martyrdom.

Avenging the nation

Selvi is driven for revenge to avenge an adopted brother's death. Sritharan, an ordinary vegetable vendor, was a caring brother to his many siblings, a duty entrusted, a power vested socially and culturally in men, a "civic" value upheld by the masculine community, as the moral police/guardians of family. Eking out a meagre living in the terror-engulfed town which had come under army control with heavy Tiger movement in the interior areas, he resolutely went about attending to his daily chore, which among others included running his modest vegetable store in the market. The town maintained a semblance of "normalcy" even though occasional skirmishes between the army and the LTTE were a frequent occurrence. While

---

[33] Benedict Anderson, *Imagined Communities* (London: Verso, 1982).
[34] Identity is about affinities based on selection, self-actualisation and choice. For Selvi, it is the notion of the preservation of her personal worth as an individual in her own right, in order to retain one's selfhood in her own eyes that becomes critical which includes among other things refusing to be inscribed the dominant identity. Struggles against subjection in cultures of terror entail often a process of destabilisation, dissolution and dissipation of identity.

the town had come under heavy army presence, the inlands were bastions of Tiger supremacy. It is impossible for civilians to escape the Tiger wrath if their orders are disobeyed. Yet they are trapped between two competing hegemonies: the army and the LTTE. Sritharan's refusal to heed the movement's warning angered the Tigers. But more importantly, it was seen as a refusal to acknowledge his ethnic identity of Tamilness and by refusing, he refused membership in the community of the Tamil "nation." By serving the army, as a Tamil of the oppressed community, he collaborates with the oppressor (Sinhalas). This exchange was seen as legitimising the army's role as an "occupying force" hell bent on destroying Tamil people, land and culture. The sole objective for which a Tamil must live and struggle for is to establish their "nation," if unachieved, relentlessly aspire to, even desire and die in the hope of that realisation. He was seen as negotiating his ethnicity in a context where identity is felt to be a prime ethnic marker. For the LTTE, Tamilness as an ethnic marker represents an "absolutism of the pure."[35] Negotiation of ethnicity or identity must be on terms set out by the movement's ideological framework. In the logic of Tamil nationalism, a national must be willing to make sacrifices in the sacred fight for freedom so that violence, as ideological practice – the will to kill/die – restores and (re)constitutes) their past greatness.[36] By daring to defy the movement's threats, he resisted the Tiger's authority to define identity, questioned the values that inform the Tamil struggle. The "unity" of the community and "stability" of identity must be maintained through persuasion, a persuasion buttressed by and impossible without coercion. United in the Tamil struggle against the Other, every Tamil must fight not just the Sinhala army or its "nation" of people, but Tamils who criticise, dissent, negate, deny their "Tamilness" and choose plural ways of realising identity.

In a culture where male valour or warfare is held supreme, acts of veeram (valour) of the sons of Eelam must be in congruence with the needs of the movement. The destruction of the Sinhala army

---

[35] Salman Rushdie, *Imaginary Homelands* (New York: Granta Books, 1991).
[36] Qadri Ismail, "Constituting nation, contesting nationalism: the Southern Tamil (women) and separatist Tamil nationalism in Sri Lanka" in *Subaltern Studies XI: Community, Gender and Violence*, eds., Partha Chatterjee and Pradeep Jeganathan (New York: Columbia University Press, 2001), 215.

helps Tamils safeguard their community, restore its lost honour; community, personal and national honour, a condition necessary for the national aspirations of Tamil people, that makes possible to move towards creating their own independent state of Tamil Eelam. By "betraying" the struggle and the community, he loses his "national" image of the vira (hero) assigned to martyrs who take an oath of loyalty to the Tamil struggle to sacrifice themselves as "suicide bombers." The conflict between ethnic subjects within a minority and antagonistic relations between them allows transformation of minority identity, which in the end generates a critique of its own condition of existence. His resistance is a critique of the movement's thrust towards normalising, hierarchising, homogenising and differentiating members of the Tamil community. In short, it is a frontal attack on the movement's intolerance for social diversity, a denial of a history of intermingling and mixing. Men's primary, or primordial task is to fulfil the demands of "nation." Members, who fail to deliver upon the promise of "nation," are assigned a different regime of valuation. As traitors, they must pay for their "crime" with death not as a sacralised symbol of purity, but a condemned cowardly criminal. The criminal, unlike the martyr, does not go through the rite de passage of 'criminalisation, politicisation and sacralisation.'[37] His resistance does not command the celebration of heroic death accorded to Tiger cadres who "brave" death. In a word, he fails to live up to the ideals of the "true martyr." His daily interaction with the Sinhala army constituted an ultimate transgression of the code of value and set of regulations governing conduct of fighting cadres in the movement. His refusal to surrender to the core constituent elements of the struggle of loyalty, obedience and a shared memory (past) is an expression of the oppositional imagination that animates those who advance the anti hegemonic struggle. Those who imagine oppositionally express their despair and anguish in poetics:

> The night
> I close my eyes
> And wanted to sleep quietly
> Eyes without sleep

---

[37] Allen Feldman, *Formations of Violence: The Narrative of The Body and Political Terror in Northern Ireland* (Chicago: Chicago University Press, 1991), 262.

Oh ! the shadows of blood

Of my brothers draped me.[38]

Selvi's resistance is motivated more or less by personal signs and symbols. She represents the Tamil notion of the woman who celebrates life, itself a negative normativity within the militarised logic of Tamil nationalism. The woman, as nurturer, has resonance that invokes respect and command in traditional patriarchal Tamil society. Shocked and shaken by the "spectacle" of punishment meted out to her brother, she goes through emotional turbulence of pain, fear, terror, anger tinged with feelings of vulnerability, insecurity, powerlessness. She invokes the ideal femininity of nurturance and affinity she cultivated with her male siblings in order not to "preserve" and "celebrate" the life of his assassin but to turn the grief and anger on him by taking his life.

In Tamil culture, masculinity is assigned superior values of fearlessness, authority, virility and aggressiveness. The notion of Tamil masculinity in the east conjures up images of men who have thunivu (courage). It is this masculine impulse that drives men to defend the home against the outside world, to brave possible or actual dangers, take action and if necessary, take to violent action.[39] The movement's humiliating treatment of her brother rids him of his masculinity depriving him of an honourable death. By returning the humiliation on his killer, Selvi returns the honour denied to the dead.[40] Unlike the Tiger women who wear a cyanide capsule[41] around their neck in the pursuit of national liberation, Selvi attempts

---

[38] Radhika Coomaraswamy, "Community, nation and militarism: Tamil nationalism in Sri Lanka" in *Pravada*. Vol. 3, No. 8, (Colombo: Social Scientists' Association, 1994), 15.

[39] Schrijvers, (1998), *op. cit.*, 33.

[40] Performing last rites to the dead is a customary cultural practice in Tamil society. The act is associated with honouring the dead, which is believed to put the soul to rest. Sangam Tamils believed that the dead did not go to either heaven or hell but resided permanently in their tombstones. There are several references to this in classical Tamil literature. Personal communication with R. Cheran 20/09/1998

[41] This is a strategy to prevent information being extracted from armed cadres in the event of arrest or capture by enemy forces. Many die instantly after consuming it. Purananuru of pre-Pallava age speaks of suicides committed by heroes. Heroic feats are not just about conquest of territory but also about cleansing the "nation." Certain suicides are committed, according to historical sources, in order to establish the honour of the warrior, a contested historical aspect privileged by writers such as Schalk in the present Tamil nationalist moment. See Schalk, *op. cit.*, 1997.

to come to terms with the reality of her brother's brutal murder driven by personal affinities with her immediate world, namely her foster family. In the quest for justice, she reconciles her nurturing self-gripped by terror and fear in her reterritorialised social space. As a female cadre, she is purported to promote the claims of the "nation" with hardened feelings of rage and bitterness, even if such rage ultimately culminates in her own self destruction. In her estimation of the ideal brother, Selvi assigns a secondary importance to her life. Her own valuation of her self worth and dignity is shifted to a different register. She values his life more than the life of a deified martyr in the movement where martyrdom is possible through negation not affirmation of life. Martyrdom, as an ideal, is achieved through means of violence and in cultures of terror such ideals acquire symbolic significance. She resolves the moral dilemma of revenge in order to affirm life, a life that was flushed out in the interest of someone else's glory. The memory of torture, abuse, sadistic laughter, dishonour, humiliation and final banishment springs forth like a flashback in her mind: they continued beating him laughing loud, insulting him, abusing him, spitting on him. In the moral resolution of the internal conflict, she becomes an instrument of death and destruction. The ideal womanhood is transformed, as Selvi becomes a gun totting, self-sacrificing aggressive woman who is willing to kill and die if necessary. Ideological discourses, argues Visweswaran, can be interrupted through individual agency. However limiting and constricting such possibilities for agency, I urge that they are contingent upon and constitutive of sociality informed by history and tradition that acquires particular hegemonic meanings in discursive regimes. Agency in ideological regimes of power as such is a disabling possibility. In exercising her negative freedom, she is nevertheless thrown to the most perilous course of action, precipitating a crisis, a crisis of a harassed self-fighting the passive self.

Yet in this violent return of the rage, Selvi's revenge in its double sense, both as conjuncture/disjuncture, converges with the demonic fury of the Tiger women who extend their anger to not just Sinhala men but her brothers and sisters in the extended Tamil family, "nation." They evoke an unbidden fear of emasculation in their capacity for violence and self annihilation. Tiger women lust for war and violence, the means by which they desire the destruction of the enemy – Sinhalas. They represent the image of the Putiya Pen (New Woman) in the Tamil nationalist/militarist project who unlike Selvi, celebrate death. Yet Selvi symbolises all that a martyr is not, what a Tiger is not. She resists threats of physical/verbal abuse and violence on her body, Tiger men's intimidations with a passive body. Violence directed at Selvi produces complexities that affect her emotionally, physically and psychologically. Such violence in patriarchal cultures is also social, classed and gendered. It is in the psychic realm, the realm of the unconscious where "duty as a sister to brother" demands that wrongs must be corrected. By fulfilling a sisterly duty, Selvi draws attention to the pervasive terror that has gripped the community. Life as a possibility derived from violence, a potentiality impregnated with brutality is constructed by the very legitimacy of violence engulfing the community in reciprocity of violence that at once divides and conflates "legitimate" from "illegitimate" violence.

In a rigid regimented military camp, in a highly militarised war zone where physical sexual intimacies are taboo, forbidden and policed, it is female bonds of solidarity that inspired intersubjective understanding between Selvi and her friend Ajitha. These instruments of sexual prohibitions are ideologically enforced in order to prevent the movement's "puritan morality" from being subverted by unauthorised sexuality in a sex/gender regime. In times of conflict, women show great resilience, courage, forge solidarities, which are nurturing and empowering. They form potential sites of subversive activity and transgressive practice. These two women often collude in secrecy and silence undermining their power, indeed domination. Ajitha had nurtured a battered Selvi emotionally during her harrowing experience of mourning the death of her brother in the absence of a body to mourn with. Selvi's inability to perform the last rites in keeping with the customary practice of burials in traditional Tamil society resulting in the denial of a decent burial for Sritharan had aggravated her emotional crisis. Ajitha's sudden disappearance, her surreptitious murder and disposal of a corpse are prompted not merely by rules of "authoritarian morality" or exigencies of militarism. Crimes of murder often targeting women illustrate the sexuality of terror within the Tiger movement. Women's sexuality, particularly its potential to swell into uncontrollable fury must be contained. If the vira stands for the defence of the preservation of the sacred "nation," women who embody the "mundane and the profane" pose an incessant threat to its "honour." While the female is appropriated as part of the "virile arsenal" of the male militant, any sign of infidelity, breach of loyalty on the part of women is singled out as treachery. By subversively, defiantly rebelling against the authority of terror of the Tigers, both women fight against their individual selves. Selvi, by turning her rage against the "brothers" of the larger kinship network, fighting her own community's terror and thereby committing an act of "treachery." Ajitha, hearing Selvi's tale of woe, decides to help a hapless woman in a hopeless, dangerous situation marked by the ubiquity of violence risking her own life. The choices both women make do not seem to alter structures of power, relations of domination/subordination, they nevertheless signify the very precariousness of conditions of domination which force them to exercise coercive choices putting their own life at risk. The sheer casualness and the chillingly cold nature of Ajitha's death is a direct outcome of the solidarity inspired by two women in a state of social crisis. While it fails to undermine the authority of the Tigers, their defiance and the dire consequences, all speak of the pervasive use of extreme violence against women within the movement, which has unremittingly relied on the conscription of young women and girls to strengthen its military stockpile.

On her return to the native village after escaping from the camp, Selvi begins to reorganise her life in the face of complete breakdown of family. Many young men and women have gone through repeated arrests and torture when members of the community pass information or give a tip off about their alleged "disappearance" from the village and the possible "past" involvement with militancy. Often, it is presumed that the "disappeared" were serving the LTTE. The community often connives with and acts in complicity with the Sinhala army or with other paramilitaries providing "information" of Tiger hideouts and areas of Tiger military presence or activity and the "civilian involvement or support" for such activity. The issue invariably involves who was serving which group and for how long. Many tip offs are handsomely rewarded while the "victims" are sent to the gallows. It is argued that the community participates in the hegemonic violence, in the network of complicity, often out of fear for their own lives. Yet, there is no denying the fact that many, uninvolved or victimised by a 'system of rules defining the permitted and the forbidden, the licit from the illicit,'[42] fall prey to such community-instigated ethnic violence. Given the paranoia and terror stalking the villagers, the survival of one depends on the annihilation of the other. Coercive apparatuses of social control of one military group are deployed in alliance with others in the community. Selvi is dependent on the good faith of a neighbour for her own survival who sends away the army when they come searching for her on information given by the villagers individually or collectively. The civilian community resorts to ruses and instruments – animosities, rivalries, prohibitions, malicious gossip, prevarication and misinformation. These govern the system of alliance, the network of surveillance, in exercising authority over the conduct of its members by naming the transgressors. The elderly neighbour not only provides her with a temporary sheltered home but also keeps the TELO militant at bay who persistently woos her for marriage. In a community where the rule of the gun reigns supreme, she boldly dismisses his sexual overtures until her re-abduction, this time by TELO, a rival armed faction of the LTTE, fighting a proxy war. Selvi is forced into womanhood, motherhood and metamorphoses into an adult woman, wife, mother, widow at a young age of fourteen. Sexuality is subsumed in alliance for all transactions – for ethnic violence, 'marriage, kinship, transactions of names and possessions.'[43] It is fear rather than choice that induces Selvi to subject herself to the lust of a man of authority. She succumbs to the pressures of his intimidations, "disciplined" by the force of "sorcery," the seductive effect of milk charmed to induce her consent. A young woman's vulnerability, in a militarised community where traditional social structures have collapsed, is greatly enhanced. Even in times of peace, coercive consent obtained from women is a telling index of patriarchal concern to exercise greater control over female sexuality. The physical constitution and the cultural construction of women as objects of male lust make them in men's eyes, potentially the more polluting of the two sexes. Women's chastity, sexual fidelity and virginity are highly valorised by

---

[42] Guha. *op. cit.*, 151.
[43] Ibid., 150.

Tamil patriarchy. Selvi loses her husband, Sengudir and also her child as she runs away from the village out of fear of the LTTE.

Selvi's transformation, from a young child of ten to an adult of fourteen at a decisive phase of Tamil nationalist struggle, is marred by a series of betrayals. Growing up as a child, she learns of the tragic and bitter "parting of ways" of her own parents, which deprived her of concern and the parental bonding that nurtures a child's formative years. The great betrayals, at a specific nationalist moment of the past in her life, constitute a symbolic field, which is suddenly overturned into a social and historical field, a battlefield and a field of struggle. It is a narrative of the great betrayal, a narrative of the social history of hegemonic nationalism, Sinhala/Tamil that emerged to bestow promises on those who had been invited to the "nation." They said they punished him for disobeying their orders...he was asked to join the movement. He refused...he was a traitor, he betrayed them...he betrayed the struggle...he betrayed the Tamil nation by collaborating with the army, the Sinhala army, he must be punished...

Restoring honour to the dead brother involves self-sacrifice, commitment, a nationalist burden imposed by Tamil patriarchy. Unlike Tiger women who make sacrifices in the name of "nation" to bring glory and victory through self-annihilation, Selvi strengthens and reaffirms the socially sanctioned patriarchal bonds that bind her to familial ties. An aspect that nevertheless reinforces and is closely tied to women's deep-seated responsibility for the well being of community, a responsibility which is a core commitment of Tamil femininity. It is at the heart of gender identity.[44] Selvi's "sacrifice," in the name of the familial, stands for profanity unlike the sacrifices of Tiger women in the interest of an illusory "nation," the ideal that symbolises sacredness and purity. Tamil "nation" denies Selvi freedom, respect and dignity. Freedom is regained by paying homage to the dead rather than a living "nation," a "nation" that differentiates between the profane and the sacred, pure/impure, martyr and the coward. Selvi's narrative of the Great Betrayals of Tamil/Sinhala nationalisms points to the very incompleteness, fragmentation and contradictory nature of collective and personal identities. A betrayal at

---

[44] Schrijvers, *op. cit.*, (1998), 32.

once couched in a feudal idiom firmly rooted in the inequality of gender relations, a nationalist idiom that appropriates ethnicity and a penal idiom legitimated in policing ethnic relations. Tamil women, like Selvi's histories, produce complexities trapped as they are in projects of identity, social demands and personal possibilities. Such histories are beyond the ken of the law. Within the ambit of the Sinhala/Tamil hegemony, Tamil woman is caught in a zero game. She cannot really be woman any more than she can be Sri Lankan like the Muslim woman in India. As woman and Sri Lankan, she cannot be Tamil. Selvi's story is of an individual, a Tamil woman, whose "minority" history has been forced out into the light of day by the enormity of social, psychic, physical and emotional violence. It is directed at her by a rupture in the 'mute complicity of horizontal loyalties'[45] in the Tamil "nation." In the unredeemed obscurity of a still active, feudal, militarised culture of terror, where Tamil women like Selvi are relentlessly and comprehensively subjected to surveillance, the only relief a woman can have is to seek relief in the interstices of society, in the crevices forgotten by weightier social forces. Not in embracing the new image of Putiya pen, Tiger women as the "masculinised other" of the male fighter. The great irony of the latter day Tamil nationalism is how it emerges as an allegory of a self in conflict with self. Both Selvi and Tiger women embody this conflict, Tiger women to a greater degree.

Armed virgins or Suthanthira
Paravaikal (Birds of Freedom) and Seductive Policing

Tiger women, as a fighting force, armed to the teeth in combat fatigues and boots with hair plaited and curled up, flaunting a cyanide capsule around their neck, marks an unprecedented change and radical departure from the dominant ideal Tamil womanhood embodying virtues of obedience and fear. While this cultural identity has been temporarily shelved and subsumed, to pave the way for a new martial[46] Tamilness, Tiger woman as the Putiya pen of Tamil

---

[45] Guha. *op. cit.*, 155.
[46] Martial traditions of the Sangam age. Modern nationalists construct a grand "martial traditions" out of feudal wars. Sangam poems are broadly divided into two sections: Aham - signifies the inner world and puram - the outer world. Inner means home, love etc. Outer represents war, politics, governance and morality. In reviving or "resurrecting" a "golden Sangam age," Tamil nationalists reconstruct history for

Eelam celebrating heroic death, represents a "martial" femininity, a femininity as a signifier of violence, a fully militarised being. In a poem written by Vanithy, a female Tiger cadre killed in battle in 1991, "She the woman of Tamililam," female fury is inserted into the semiotics of Tamil nationalism, a deviation fuelled, encouraged and often imposed by nationalist hatred/lust for war and brutality.

> Her forehead should be adorned not with
> Kumkum[47] (but) with red blood
> all that is seen in her eyes is not the sweetness
> of youth (but) firm declarations of those
> who have fallen down
> On her neck will lay no Tali (but) a cyanide flask !
> her legs are going and searching
> not for searching a relationship with relatives
> (but) looking towards the liberation of
> the soil of Tamililam
> her gun will fire shots
> no failure will cause the enemy to fall !!
> it will break the fetters of Tamililam !!
> then from our people's lips a national anthem
> will tone up !![48] (my emphasis)

In the formation of a new martial identity for women, Tamil nationalism takes control over traditions to be reauthorised and re-

---

deployment in its present day glorification of nationalist violence. Ironically, in the martial ideology of Tamil nationalism, the *maravar*, (warrior) is exclusively a male, the new "national" privileged in Tamil nationalism. It is interesting yet to see how martial ideology is deployed in making nationalist appeals to women. The concept of "martial feminism" has been developed by several theoreticians of Tamil nationalism to explain the extraordinary phenomenon of militancy of Tamil women. Chief among them is Peter Schalk of Uppsala, a campaigner for Tamil separatism. According to Schalk, Tiger women's new role as armed combatants is a revolutionary step, an indication of the radicalisation of the socially conservative Tamil society. Central to the goals of martial feminism is mobilisation of women into the military structures of the LTTE, a move I argue, that serves the material interests of the movement and its continued ideological control of women. Schalk's views have been criticised by several scholars.

[47] Kumkum or kumgumam is red powder applied in the form of pottu. Usually married women wear kumgumam or vermillion on their forehead.

[48] See the chapter "Victim or Agent?: The Sri Lankan militant woman in the interregnum," in Neloufer de Mel, *Women in The Nation's Narrative: Gender and Nationalism in the Twentieth Century Sri Lanka*, (New Delhi: Kali for Women, 2004).

constituted. In this new disciplinary reordering of Tamil cultural moral universe, certain traditions are singled out and systematically repudiated. Instead of heterosexual marriage, death is consummated, a condition that makes possible the emergence of the new nation, the very process of nation formation. Tiyakam (abandonment of life) is achieved through katpu (chastity) and arpanippu (sacrifice). The female militant retains chastity and purity in death; 'In her self-image, she dies pure and heroically.'[49] The Tiger woman glorifies martyrdom and death, spurns bourgeois marriage and condemns a life of drudgery and victimisation. Social/familial ties and extended networks have been replicated with communal ties welded together and hemmed in by a jungle-based guerrilla life. The ironical twist in new Tamilness is how the Tiger women's new "freedom" in the Tamil "nation" is transferred from one variation of patriarchal dominance to another. In this reconstitution of patriarchy, there is no promise of ensuring 'Tamil women control their own lives'[50] as promulgated by the LTTE Women's Front in 1991. The cultural and ethnic markers have been replaced with the blood of and violence against the vanquished inscribing the new "nation." The blood of her vanquished will crown her in glory. Blood constitutes one of the fundamental values in a class/caste differentiated Tamil society. It has its instrumental role. The instrumentality has its own precariousness. It also has a certain function in the order of signs. Seeing the bleeding body of her brother, Selvi hastens to take revenge, prepares to risk her blood. Revenge in the form of spilling the blood of her brother's assassin becomes a form of purification in which the impure body of her brother is sacralised. For Tiger women, the expiation of the violated body achieves two objectives; the purification of the body (the woman's) and the purification of the "nation," the social body. The ostensibly "pregnant" woman who rammed into the vehicle carrying state representatives in Jaffna in January 1996 killing several in-

---

[49] Peter Schalk. "Birds of Independence: On the participation of Tamil women in armed struggle" *in Ilankai*, 7, (Uppsala University, 1992), 44-142

[50] Women's Front of the LTTE also aims to abolish oppressive caste discrimination, social divisions and semi feudal customs such as the dowry system, secure legal protection for women against sexual harassment, rape and domestic violence. See Schalk, "Women fighters of the liberation tigers in Tamil Eelam: The martial feminism of Atel Palacinkam," in *South Asia Research* Vol. 14. No. 2, (1994), 169.

stantly and injuring others, was an instance of purification of the
"nation." Dhanu[51], a victim of gang rape by Indian forces, blew her
self up garlanding the former Prime Minister of India, Rajiv Gandhi.
According to Tiger propaganda, she performed, simultaneously, a
purificatory ritual to rid the body of all impurities as a result of rape
by the Indian army. The Tiger women's satitva (the oath of loyalty)
resonates with the Hindu woman's wifely virtues of truthfulness or
fidelity to her husband. Here, the Tamil woman's sacrifice is offici-
ated not through the ritual of marriage. Her final journey is sacralised by political sanction. In the glorification of the Tiger practice of
suicide, it is the woman's endurance as well as "nation"s continuity
that becomes the signifier of value, both derived from painful acts of
veeram. It is this desire of pain that serves as an index of Tamil
women's cultural even racial superiority and as an absolute signifier
of "difference" in the Tamil "nation."[52] There is effective ideological
manipulation of the sexual/national body achieved through "agency"
of political violence, biological defilement, purifying sacrificial death
and political sacralisation.'[53] Tiger women rejoice death with a "martyr's pride. This new gender identity is pitted against not just men but
against other women. So that women become women not only in
relation to men but also in relation to other women.[54] Here tradition
comes into conflict with modernity. Selvi's struggle to preserve her
family members based on nostalgia and sentimentality as opposed to
Tiger women's desire to preserve the purity of the struggle based on
denial. It is those very traditional familial social bonds and cultural
values in Tamil society embodied in Tamil womanhood, the LTTE
exploits, to mobilise young women into the movement. In a culture
under attack, the good woman as the repository of community and

---

[51] Dhanu was believed to have been gang raped by Indian Peace Keeping Forces
(IPKF) during their violent confrontation with the LTTE between 1987-1990 in
Jaffna. She was subsequently "groomed" by the Tigers to assassinate the former PM
of India, Rajiv Gandhi, who in their perception was responsible for sending Indian
troops to disarm Tamil militants that eventually led to a bloody conflict followed by
massacres of civilians, rape of women and plunder of villages.
[52] Sunder Rajeswari Rajan, *Real and Imagined Women: Gender, Culture and Post-
colonialism*, (London: Routledge, 1993), 22.
[53] A Feldman, *Formations of Violence*, (1991), 265.

family honour struggles to preserve the value of her tradition. Many in the community see how the Tigers harness these very values; 'She joins her brother who is dying for a cause. She feels she must go and help him. Not only just her brother but also her father, neighbour, the village men, the village women, the area men, the region men, the whole community. When a woman joins the movement, she knows she is going to die. But she is fully satisfied. She thinks I bring credit to my family this way. I know I die but it is good for our family and it is good for our community.'[55] Many women joined the LTTE when their own brother, father or husband were killed or disappeared during the early years of the armed conflict. Many young girls and boys came from families affected by ethnic violence in the absence of male breadwinner. The movement, however regularly, conscripts, forcibly and routinely recruit youth as war soldiers, boys and girls into its military fold.

In the nationalist mobilisation of the new woman, it is Kali's image and Kali's malevolence that Tiger women appropriate in the nationalist punitappor (sacred war) to protect the tayakam (motherland). Like Kannagi[56] who summoned her female powers of chastity (katpu) and cut her left breasts and burned the city of Madurai, Tiger women are invited to use their katpu for destructive ends. This image of the putiya pen as the poem illustrates is hindered and exalted by ambiguities. As Tamil women's identity is defined in relation to her family, community and "nation," the female profane nature merges

[54] The idea is K. Visweswaran's. "Small speeches, subaltern gender: Nationalist ideology and its historiography," *Subaltern Studies IX.*, eds., Shahid. Amin & Dipesh. Chakrabarty (New Delhi: Oxford University Press, 1996).

[55] Schrijvers, "Constructing `womanhood,' `Tamilness' and `the refugee': internal refugees in Sri Lanka" in *Women, Narration and Nation*, ed., Selvi Thiruchandran New Delhi: Vikas Publications, 1999), 180.

[56] In Shilappadikaram (Tamil epic) of the Sangam age, Kovalan was married to the beautiful Kannagi, but he spent all his wealth on the dancing girl Madhavi. After a quarrel with Madhavi, he returns penniless to his wife. Together they set out for Madurai where Kovalan hoped to sell Kannagi's anklet. A goldsmith who had stolen a similar anklet belonging to the Pandiya queen accused Kovalan of the theft. Pandiya king believed his false testimony and ordered Kovalan's execution. Kannagi challenges the Pandiya king when he unjustly executed her husband Kovalan. The king dies of grief at the injustice he had committed. Furious, and not satisfied with justice, Kannagi summons her female energy of "chastity," (*katpu*) tears off her left breast, throws it and burns the city of Madurai. In popular Tamil nationalist discourse, Kannagi gets equated to women with *katpu*.

with the sacred maram (valour) of the vira. Her terror is akin to the destructive powers of Kali who is commonly imaged in terrifying manner; Red eyes, dishevelled hair, blood trickling at the corners of her mouth, lips saturated with fresh blood, a dangling tongue, long sharp fangs, a gaunt dark skinned body, a sunken stomach and protruding breasts. Her necklace contains fifty human heads; her waistband is a girdle made of severed human arms. She wears two dead infants for earrings.[57] In her many manifestations, Kali is also worshipped as the source of power, strength, equality and justice. In the Tiger adulation of Kali, like bloodthirstiness as the evocative verses of Vanithy signify, Tiger woman is represented as out of control both on and off the battlefield. It is the image of the female fury that is fetishised into productive commodity by male Tigers, their delight and hubris in death and destruction. They completely efface out woman as the 'incarnation of ahimsa.'[58] In its negative representation of the ideal as both out of control and destructive, Tiger woman is denied the value assigned to the male warrior. In Tamil nationalist idiom then, the female Tiger cadre cannot be a true martyr/warrior. For Selvi, there is a certain "rejoice" in the ending of dishonour. The desire of revenge (in order to preserve life) is a counterpoise to the Tiger women's desire of emasculation as new forms of bondage of patriarchy in its dual role of the cynical national and the authoritarian "nation."

Manipulating motherhood

In many acts of subversion and protest of women, there is acceptance of the hierarchies of power. There is also challenge and in some, there is realignment of the symbols to serve their own interests. Tiger women proudly flaunt their own self-image of the emancipated putiya pen, an image different from that of reticent, dutiful sisters, wives and daughters. This image is constructed in opposition to the chaste Tamil wife who must enter monogamous marriage in order to produce future sons of Eelam. They embody the emerging "nation" of a martial race and Tamil culture personifying veeram

---

[57] Lina Gupta, "Kali the saviour" in *After Patriarchy: Feminist Transformations of The World Religions*, eds.., Paula M Cooey (New York: Orbis Books, 1992), 20-21.
[58] Nita Kumar, ed., *Women As Subjects: South Asian histories* (Charlottesville: University Press of Virginia, 1994), 44.

and thyagam (sacrifice). As M(others) of the "nation," the Tamil militant mother incites the son to take up arms when the "nation" is in
conflict. Drawing from the historical tradition[59] and in the war poems of Purananuru[60], the image reclaimed is the woman, who having
lost her father and husband in battle, turns to her son, gives him a
spear to hold, turns his face to the battle and urges him to go.[61] Yet
women are mere adjuncts to the larger nationalist struggle. War, as
male lust for power, demands male sacrifices for tayakam (motherland) to be liberated; 'For the birth of the motherland, father and son
must die.'[62] There is no recognition of female sacrifices. The great
irony of Tamil nationalist practice today is how Tamil women are
made to transgress constraining bonds of motherhood to be warriors
themselves. The image of the woman in early Tamil history is a female inciter to violence, a passive role. Tamil nationalism reinterprets
this history to assign women an active role. A popular drawing discursively deployed by nationalists graphically portrays a mother,
young son and an elderly woman (a mother-in-law) at the sepulchre
of the slain father-husband-son. The woman hands over an AK 47 of
the husband to the son. Tiger movement's re-appropriation of the
metaphor of mother constitutes a realm of duality and ambiguity.
Not all mothers are given membership into the "nation." Those who
enter must allow their pain and anger associated with death or dis-

[59] C. S. Lakshmi refers to such a tradition in classical Tamil poetry. The idea that
women's wombs become "liars of tigers" from which emerge sons majestic like tigers
who go to the battlefield has persisted and continues to be a dominant element in
Tamil nationalism. Poems from Puarananuru (songs of valour) abound in such idealised images. Ironically most such poems on heroic mothers are by women poets.
Verses of maternal valour often evoke images of erotic violence; "If he really broke
down/ in the thick of battle/I'll slash these breasts that gave him suck." Another goes;
"She rummaged through/the blood red field/till she found her son/quartered in
pieces/and she rejoiced/more than the day/she gave him birth." See Lakshmi, *op. cit.*,
1990, 72. Lakshmi argues when nationalism is in conflict, nationalists discursively
construct women's bodies as sites of divinity, sanctity and purity where all societal
notions of life and living seem to converge enduring their bodies with some mystical
qualities. This makes them "naturally" produce "milk of valour" for their sons to
infuse in their blood bravery and courage to become warriors.
[60] An ancient classic depicting heroic (sic) exploits of various Tamil kings. The poems
belong to Sangam period (300 B.C – 200 A.D)
[61] Peter Schalk, "Heroisation of the martial ideology of the LTTE" in *South Asia*, Vol.
XX No. 2 (1997), 57.
[62] Schalk, *op. cit.*, 58.

appearance of male relatives to be used to ideological effect. Pupathi[63], the moral Tamil mother from the eastern province staged a hunger strike in protest against killings of young men in the North and East in 1989 by the The Indian Peace Keeping Force (IPKF) during their peacekeeping operations in Sri Lanka. She sustained her fast until her death for which she was elevated to the status of a martyr by the LTTE. The heroisation of Pupathi as veerathai (heroic mother) resonates with mythic history of the Sangam period.

The veerathai, adulated in LTTE nationalist text, is a Tamil mother who takes pride over her martyred son's death. Such adulation is the means by which nationalist heroised mothers are mobilised to perpetuate political violence. Yet Pavalamma, as Tamil mother of three sons, is unable to claim her identity as veerathai since two of her sons are members of a rival militant group fighting the hegemony of the LTTE. The tragic story of Pavalamma was unearthed by a group[64] working underground to document human rights abuses in the north and east. Much of the contents in their report focused on individual abuses at the hands of the LTTE, members of the Sri Lankan armed forces and various paramilitary groups. The description on Pavalamma was brief and terse. UTHR records;

'Pavalamma from Chavakachcheri was arrested in Jaffna in 1990. Widowed mother of three sons, two of who were members of EPRLF, a rival militant group of the LTTE. The Tiger women removed all her jewellery and cash claiming they are stolen property. She was kept manacled and locked throughout her captivity in the torture camp. She was forced to bathe off water in a drum under observation and repeatedly beaten, forced to pass under barbed wire, made to witness other women being assaulted; middle aged and grandmothers hung from pulleys; bleeding women made to stand in the sun without water. Pavalamma was thrown on the ground and trampled with booted feet each time she "refused to tell the truth."

---

[63] Tamil women in the North and East came out strongly against atrocities and violations of human rights resorting to mostly non-violent forms of agitation. They formed themselves into a "Mother's Front" publicly campaigning against brutalities of the Sinhala army and the repression of Tamils by the Sinhala state in the early 80s. During the mid 80s, Pupathi fasted to death against the presence of the Indian forces. She was martyred by the LTTE.

[64] The University Teachers of Human Rights, Jaffna (www.uthr.org).

When she began bleeding, she was made to wash the blood off the floor. Melted wax poured on her hands...confession extracted and falsified. She was sent for manual labour – to build bunkers.'[65] (My emphasis)

Tamil nation inflicts unspeakable acts of cruelty on Pavalamma for investing her maternal instincts in a political project of protest. In the lived nation of Tamil Eelam, the heroic mother becomes heroic in relation to her sons who not only must be virile and brave but virility must be nurtured in the community of Tamile Eelam. As non-members of Tamileelam, they become men lacking in virility. Yet she resists the attempts to destroy her consolidated will to relent, to be intimidated by acts of terror, to be shamed into subjection, to be imposed a life of living death in a ghetto of inexorable violence and in resisting, refuses to claim the pride of common martyrdom accorded for mothers for producing brave sons of Tamil Eelam. Shoot me if you will! In this act of defiance, in struggling against a culture of terror being foisted on her, Pavalamma struggles against the power of naming her as Tamilthay of traitors. The stability of gender identity is maintained based on differences between women as a group: the LTTE mother vs. non-LTTE or anti LTTE mother. Mothers of Tiger women privately share their pride of being mothers of heroic daughters who have achieved positions of power and authority driving their armoured jeeps and displaying their military prowess. Pavalamma, the "moral [O]ther" has shame and guilt to save herself from the stigma of a "demeaned" motherhood. The consequential effect of the "Great Denials"[66] attributed to Pavalamma in the community of Tamil nation unfurls how a woman's erasure is sublimated over the construction of a momentous event, to be silenced and erased in nationalist history. The embodied violence against Pavalamma constitutes an "unforgettable event"[67] in the collective memory of Tamil community's experience in a specific geographic space of North and East. A place in a historical relation-

---

[65] *UTHR*, 8/3/1995.
[66] The fragment is from Shahid Amin, "Remembering Chauri Chaura: Notes from historical fieldwork" in *Subaltern Studies Reader*, ed., Ranajit Guha (University of Minnesota Press, 1998).
[67] Shahid Amin, *Event, Metaphor, Memory: Chauri Chaura 1922-1992*, (Berkeley: University of California Press, 1998), 9.

ship of power, a relationship of male dominance maintained by ethnicity; 'There are things heard, seen and experienced which no self respecting woman can bear to repeat and moreover under no circumstances should any woman be exposed to such things...This experience constantly gives me great pain. I can not believe that it happened to me, an ordinary housewife and mother, I keep wondering if it were all a dream...'

A new female commander recognising her as a native of the same village, later released Pavalamma, when the senior female Tiger cadre, who personally inflicted torture on her, was transferred to another prison. Pavalamma returned to a refugee camp in a village, in the east after her release, continuing her search for the missing sons. If Selvi's sense of grief and shock at the sight of her brother's brutal murder was redeemed by an intrepid solidarity - Ajitha aiding Selvi fully to inure the task of revenge - Pavalamma's experience of the materiality of violence in the Tamil "nation" was physically brought to an end by a Tiger woman, a "solidarity" based on a contradictory principle, a "solidarity" nevertheless inspired by a shared historical understanding. Both forms of solidarity and the very conflicting ways in which the choice of solidarity asserted is a measure of both the contingency and complexity of the conditions under which they find themselves in. Pavalamma's maternal defiance like Selvi's revenge is deeply subversive of Tamil nationalism. While the subversion is never complete or partially achieved, these discordant, fragile and marginal solidarities expose the movement's pretensions to kinship ties of comradeship and break the myth of the "nationals" as a community of cohesive and non antagonistic relations. The poignant life story of Pavalamma, her recalcitrance in the face of great odds, her resilience and resistance in a militarised society where the brute force of patriarchy is inescapable and unabated, highlights moments that have the potential of being disruptive and must be seen as such. They ought to be recognised as ruptures, as patriarchy's momentary retreat in the face of a woman's determination to assert control over her own body, in order to capture sites of alternative visions of freedom.

Fictions of homogeneity

Among the Ten Commandments, issued by the militants in 1985 all over Jaffna in the northern peninsula under the rubric

"Warning to Women," many socially restrictive injunctions were imposed on them; 'Married women should wear sarees when going out; do not wear nighties and transparent clothes; women who loiter about in public places should be beaten; parents, who allow their grown up daughters to behave as they like, should be punished and disgraced.'[68] Central to the system of social and ideological control of femininity and female sexuality is the notion of Tamil womanhood constructed in a binary opposition; the Tamil woman who embodies Kali in her vengeful, malevolent form and Amman[69] (female goddess) simple, mild and chaste. Both forms suggest an active sexuality that needs to be regulated and contained.

The entry of women into the movement, in its initial recruitment stages, aroused mixed feelings of anxiety and scorn especially among women in the community. Older women in particular took a hard line attitude. They were virulently harsh and critical of the younger women. The induction of women into a movement, in a society 'hierarchically organised and seeped in the ideology of male dominance,' marked a turning point. Increasing state repression, widespread sexual violence against women followed by disappearance and displacement led to large-scale recruitment drives by the LTTE. The push was circumstantial and material rather than ideological. Such a rupture was far from real since the 'women's position is shaped in every aspect...by a girdle of patriarchy.' In the ensuing years, with the age of marriage rapidly rising and dowry prices spiralling, young women from the east were compelled to join the movement. In the north, nationalist appeals made to women's `deep-felt responsibility for the well-being of the community' drew them in large numbers into the military fold of the LTTE. The hostility of older women as well as men in the community towards younger women's seduction by a `narrow, revivalistic and romantic' thrust of a movement, 'well-sprinkled with images of male heroes and male valour,' was not a reaction based on the reality of patriarchy's bid to compromise women's interests in the altar of "nation." But rather the degree of "danger" female sexuality posed to the realisation of that

---

[68] Schrijvers, *op. cit.*, (1998), 32.
[69] Amman is a general name for female goddess in the Hindu pantheon. Kali is a form of Amman.

ideal. Older women used the existing sexual hierarchies to vilify the younger women flocking in numbers to the movement; 'Tigers were all right till women joined them. They have spoilt the movement and the boy's dedication.'[70] Professional women in the community, as "archetypes" of sexual morality, were spouting out equally prurient derisive remarks. Outraged at declining morality in Tamil society, upper class women snapped arrogantly; 'those days when we asked these women why they joined the movement, they said that it was for the sake of our land. Now where is the land? Why could these women have not kept quiet? They are the ones who give all the encouragement to the men.'[71] Such patriarchal prohibitions and purificatory rules were traditionally enforced to ensure the safety of the social body from sexual pollution since women were capable of such pollution as they are primarily defined as "wives, mothers and "distractors of men" from doing their manly duties.'[72] Arguably, women occupy purifying/defiling spaces in the Tamil "nation" as sacrificial martyrs or sexually disembodied selves. Women consciously or unconsciously have perpetuated this material and cultural policing in a collective project in which subordination of women is historically sustained. There is physical (outer) and moral (inner self) control of female powers in Tamil society. In creating a new military citizenry, there is a clear shift of power and authority from the traditional nuclear family to the collective Tamil Eelam family. This erosion of power from one domain leads to the consolidation of power in another. In 1996, Tiger men publicly executed three women alleged to have premarital sexual relations outside the movement. There is a vast conspiracy of silence on the movement's attitude towards and treatment of women, on sexual abuse, abortion, divorce and prostitution; 'The movement banned abortion in order to control women's reproductive choices that would hamper its efforts in mobilising youth into its ranks in the interest of moral purity.'[73]

---

[70] Rajan Hoole et. al., *The Broken Palmyrah: The Tamil Crisis in Sri Lanka. An Inside Account.* (Claremont, Ca.: Sri Lanka Studies Institute, 1990), 327.

[71] *op. cit.* , 829.

[72] C.S Lakshmi, *The Face Behind The Mask: Women in Tamil Literature.* (New Delhi, Vikas Publications, 1984), 3.

[73] Interview with Parvati Kanthasamy, Toronto, 26/12/1995.

Violence against women in the Tamil nation, as the stories of Selvi and Pavalamma well illustrate, grounds the deep-seated culturally infused hatred and fear of women endemic in Sri Lankan society. In times of crisis, relations of power, which heighten such fears, congeal into hegemonies. They tend to "serve" the interests of the dominant regime since such relations are capable of being utilised in strategies. Such dynamics, Foucault calls the 'most speculative, most ideal, the most internal element in a deployment of sexuality organised by power in its grip on bodies and their materiality.'[74] Will the feudal ideology in a radically transformed Tamil social formation that has seen a "subversion" of cultural values dissipate altogether creating effective cracks in the ideology of Tamil womanhood? There is scepticism and apprehension, among some, that repressive sexual practices might resurface; 'in a new reordering of Tamil society, dominant sexual taboos will re-emerge with diminished prospects of marriage and family life. There will be some equality once peace returns to the North and East. Ex-cadres will experience the burden of stigma. Men will not be willing to marry them.'[75] Patriarchy will let men off the hook and escape social sanction. Ex-militant women, constrained by a life of prolonged detention, too voice their concerns. They express concern for safety of relatives and family members and do not care or have any regard for Eelam or Sri Lanka. Like the women who fear for the young children being forced away from their care to be drafted as fighters and the traumatised mother who grieves, in private, for her daughter killed in a bomb explosion set on alert for enemy infiltration. Yet, Tiger women are symbolically integral to the armed struggle and continue to be instrumentally constitutive of the shared imaginary of the dominant cultural order.

State as perpetrator

To return to the story of Selvi, the law's concern in assigning criminality to her as a "defendant" in the "case" against her by the State, her re-abductor, vindicates the legitimacy of the hegemonic power of Sinhala/Tamil nationalist enterprise that ruthlessly perpetuates a system of domination based on a "morality" of violence.

---

[74] Judith Butler, "Variations on Sex and Gender: Beauvoir, Wittig and Foucault" in *Feminism as Critique*, eds., Sheila Benhabib & Drucilla Cornell (London: Polity Press, 1987), 139.
[75] Interview with D.B.S. Jeyaraj, (Toronto, 27/12/1995).

Caught between these two intrusive forces of power, women like Selvi and Pavalamma whose resistance takes the "noncollective" or "unorganised"[76] form, defy 'the ruse of law and confer their story, the dignity of an adversarial discourse.'[77] In dignifying her text, Selvi reclaims her life through narrative. Her subversive resistance, transgressive defiance is the site of actual and symbolic struggle in spite of the collusion, convergence and complicity. For without even marginally being complicit, women cannot arguably invert the negative value system that sustains the consent of a community gripped by systematic domination. Individual biography and collective history seem united at least momentarily as history and the body become each others' terrain.[78] The struggles of Selvi and Pavalamma, a hitherto "devalued and neglected"[79] form of resistance is directed at two regimes of power which co-exist and intertwine in contemporary Tamil society; power vested in individual men and men as a group. The ground for resistance waged on the level of the particular and the historical for women poses limitations for emancipatory potential of politics. Their transgressive resistance remodifies power's hold on them as domains of power relations in their own right, they 'serve to discipline as well as to formulate patterns of resistance.'[80] It neither transforms the dominant networks of power nor frees them from their own oppressive condition.

In "remembering" and recalling "memory" of lived experience, Selvi's narrative throws open not just the relationship of resistance to power but the very specificity of the norms and forms of domination. It provokes one to rethink the Foucauldian formulation 'where there is power, there is resistance, and yet, rather consequently, this resistance is never in a position of exteriority in relation to power.'[81] Selvi's narrative makes us reverse Foucault's provocative

---

[76] Lila Abu-Lughod, "The romance of resistance: Tracing transformations of power through Bedouin women" in *The American Ethnologist*, (February 1990) 17 (1), 41.

[77] Guha. *op. cit.*, 161.

[78] Fernando Coronil & Julie Skurski, "Dismembering and remembering the nation: the semantics of political violence in Venezuela" in *Comparative Studies in Society and History*, 33 (2), (April 1991), 290.

[79] Abu-Lughod, *op. cit.*,41.

[80] James C. Scott, *Domination and The Arts of Resistance*, (London: Yale University press), 1990, 118.

[81] Scott. *op. cit.*, 111.

insight to discern its full significance; 'Where there is resistance, there is power or power is never in a position of exteriority in relation to resistance.' Selvi's revenge, in the end, is a [un]consciously adopted strategy to prevent the surviving members of her foster family fall prey to Tiger terror, to fight for her right to a life with dignity within her own society. To stop the machine of terror from uprooting a woman from her place in the local community, a community where Tamil nationalisms' moral authority stands so clearly opposed to her interests, to women's interests. An act of resistance against a hideous patriarchal tradition of routine violence of slaughter that took Ajitha's life, among its other unseen victims. The 'struggle against power, Rushdie reminds us, is a struggle of memory against forgetting.'[82] Yet her resistance took that characteristic form, often adopted by the oppressed, to subvert the designs of her oppressors in the guise of conforming to them. Her story lays bare the limits of solidarity that homogenises the members of the "nation." The loudest protest against violence in the Tamil "nation" is articulated in the domain of an alternative solidarity, however fragile, solidarity of women. In "remembering" the small events of Tamil nationalist history and the tragic trajectory of an ordinary woman 'journeying, as we all journey, down little, but unforgettable roads'[83], both Selvi and Pavalamma, in their limited ways, step into the role of critic, a systemic critic, of the culture that brutalises them. Yet from their critique there flow the elements of practice of resistance, a resistance at once limited but necessary yet flawed. It is critical to recall Proust here who once remarked: 'People foolishly imagine that the broad generalities of social phenomena afford an excellent opportunity to penetrate further into the human soul; they ought, on the contrary, to realize that it is by plumbing the depths of a single personality that they might have a chance of understanding those phenomena.'[84]

Can the subversive potential of women, caught between the desire of a world of dignity and freedom and the reality of a seductive appeal of the "nation," actually undermine the hegemonic nationalist narrative? The discursive imperative of the narrative text is

---

[82] S. Rushdie, *op. cit.*, 1991, 36.
[83] *op. cit.* 42.

to question the very constitution of the nation, the construction of the nationalist narrative. It further argues how the fluidity of women's position and experience makes it difficult and dangerous to homogenise experience of "small" narratives. The intimate story, not the grand epic, reveals a different story, a different sense of the Historical, a new sense of the Political that defies the teleology of History. Selvi, a young woman orphaned, adopted, abducted, raped and transformed into a murderous partisan all in the name of patriarchy; family, "nation" and community. What is she in the end? Who is she? And what is her role in Sri Lanka's future social formation? Victim? Agent? Terrorist? Militant? If her resistance forms a struggle of redefining the ideological basis of the nationalist war, her story does not end but begins with the ethico-political questioning: Who has the right to remember? And the right to imagine?

Mangalika de Silva *is a PhD student of anthropology at the Amsterdam School for Social Science Research (ASSR,) University of Amsterdam, in the Netherlands.*

---

[84] Marcel Proust, *In Search of Lost Time*. Vol 3. (Trans.) C.K. Scott Moncrieff & T. Kilmartin (New York: Modern Library, 1993).

Ethnic differences and urban neighbourhood relationships among slum dwellers of Colombo.

Niriellage Chandrasiri Niriella

ABSTRACT

The present paper on urban low-income neighbourhoods mainly focuses on the 1983 riot affected areas in the City of Colombo. Various kind of information proved that, except the Tamil people living in the slum neighbourhoods, a significant number of the Tamils in the Colombo City were affected by the violence or harassed by mobs in July 1983. The prolonged ethnic social strife in this small country has continuously produced tension and stressful life among various social classes of residents in the city. In relation to this, the study mainly focuses attention on the way in which the slum people manage to live together despite ethnic differences in their neighbourhoods. The study focused on two-selected slum neighbourhoods in Colombo City. The slum is not only the place where people live; there is some mutual understanding and intimate social relationships. People of both the slums displayed their political awareness of the ethnic social strife in the country. More than 85 percent of the residents in the both neighbourhoods stated that "discussion" was the main solution for the ethnic conflict. One of the important findings is the positive attitude among the residents towards inter-ethnic marriages and neighbour relations. Other major positive thinking on neighbour relations was that residents of both the neighbourhoods stated that they face no problems with persons of other ethnic groups being a member of his/her association as personal chums, street neighbours, co-occupation colleagues, and as citizens of the country. Overall, in spite of minor set backs and prejudices, the residents of the both the communities show remarkable resilience towards ethnic groups and strive to maintain peace and harmony in their neighbourhoods. There are several positive forces bringing social cohesion than disruptive forces (like crime and political maneuvers) affecting friendly environment in the settlements under present focus. If given financial support, they would like to move to other residential areas but far better economic status and not due to inter-ethnic biases.

Domains 2: 54 – 75 | Copyright © 2005 South Focus Press

The concept of the neighbourhood[1] finds a prominent place in contemporary urban policy and research. The neighbourhood provides an useful scale for studying social relationships of 'everyday life-worlds.'[2] Also there is a longstanding interest in the residential neighbourhood in western sociology. From the early Chicago School onwards, sociologists such as Suttles[3] and Fischer[4] have been concerned with processes of adaptation and associations in cities and significance of neighbours, friends and neighbourhoods in the shaping of opportunities and social divisions. In contemporary policy debates in the USA and Europe, there is a renewed interest in the neighbourhood as a key domain for the transmission of shared values and norms and as essential building block for wider social cohesion.[5] Also, the neighbourhood remains the major site for enforcement of safety in public space, for the respect of norms of commonality, for collective socialisation of children, for grassroots initiatives, in brief, for the expression of a shared social capital.[6]

Typically, a neighbourhood is a sufficiently compact, area of living, which permits frequent and fairly intimate contacts between its members. Social interaction in a neighbourhood is face-to-face and primary. This makes for a strong sense of togetherness, ensures conformity to group norms, and endows every member with the capacity to influence behaviour of others. Thus understood, a neighbourhood presupposes a degree of homogeneity, stability of residence and restricted physical mobility away from the community, factors that are hardly likely to be found in urban communities. The intimate neighbourhood seems to belong to the village or small town.

---

[1] Neighbourhood is defined as follows: it is the bundle of spatially based attributes associated with clusters of residences, social character, unity or belonging, and local facility use etc. Sometimes they are in conjunction with other usages

[2] A. Kearns, and M. Parkinsion, "The Significance of Neighbourhood," in *Journal of Urban studies*, vol. 38, no. 12. (2001), pp 2103-2110.

[3] Gerald Suttles, *The Social Construction of Communities.* (Chicago: University of Chicago Press, 1972)

[4] C. Fischer, *To Dwell Among Friends: Personal Networks in Town and City*, (Chicago: University of Chicago Press).

[5] R.Forrest, A.L. Grange, and Y.N. Ming, *Neighbourhood in a High Rise, High Density: Some Observations on Contemporary Hong Kong*, (Oxford: The Editorial Board of the Sociological Review & Blackwell Publishers 2002).

[6] Sophie Body-Gendrot, *The Social Control of Cities.* (Oxford: Blackwell Publishers, 2000).

The spatial patterns of cities, multi-storeyed apartment buildings, density and heterogeneity of the population, continuous shifts of residence are characteristics one normally associates with the city and these are hardly conducive to the intimate face-to-face contacts of neighbourhood life. Individual neighbourhoods are certainly a fact of city life but this may be a physical rather than a social fact.[7] However, some classical literature on 'community' and 'neighbourhood' show that inner city areas, especially in the US, exhibited primary ties with tight social bonds, social networks, and strong institutional forms among urban people.[8]

Many scholars on slums[9] emphasise the 'anti-social' nature of slums. They describe slums as a place generally associated with problems such as crime, delinquency, prostitution, gambling and regard them as a special type of disorganised and disintegrated area. Contrary to this notion, there are classic sociological studies of slums reveal that the slum is well knit and organised. Many scholars have rejected negative assumptions about the urban poor i.e., that they suffer from a culture of poverty, that slum life is socially disorganised and that there is a duality between the slum and non-slum people. They confirm the existence of organised social and political life among slum dwellers.

It would be relevant to examine the efficacy of the 'neighbourhood' concept in the context of Sri Lankan society, more

---

[7] M.S. Gore, *In-Migrants and Neighbourhoods: Two Aspects of Life in a Metropolitan City.* (Deonnar, Bombay: Tata Institute of Social Sciences, 1970).

[8] William. F. Whyte, *Street Corner Society: The Social Structure of an Italian Slum.* (Chicago: The University of Chicago Press, 1943); P.Young and M. Willmott, *Family and Class in a London Suburb.* (London: Routledge and Kegan Paul, 1962); J. Herbert Gans, *The Urban Villagers: Group and Class in Life of Italian-Americans.* (New York: The Free Press of Glencoe, 1962); Gerald Suttles, *The Social Construction of Communities.* (Chicago: University of Chicago Press, 1972) & *The Social Order of Slum.* (Chicago: The University of Chicago Press, 1968); Suzanne Keller, *The Urban Neighbourhood.* (New York: Random House, 1968); Barry Wellman and Barry Leighton, (1979) "Networks, Neighbourhoods, and Communities" in *Approaches to the Study of the Community Question*, eds., Ronald L. Warren and Larry Lyon (1983) & *New Perspectives on the American Community.* (Illinois: The Dorsey Press, 1983), 246 - 262.

[9] A 'slum' is an inner-city neighbourhood characterized by high density housing units that are deteriorated permanent structures. Also, it refers to cramped, squalid, poorly endowed living areas, found in economically, socially, psychologically and politically deprived urban regions.

specifically in the case of slum localities in the city of Colombo. Sri Lankan society has been legitimately termed multi-racial, multi-ethnic, multi-religious, and multi-lingual comprising of as it does, mainly three distinct ethnic groups – Sinhala, Tamils (Sri Lankan Tamils, Indian Tamils), and Muslims who follow four of the principal religions of the world viz. Buddhism, Hinduism, Islam and Christianity. The Sinhalese form the majority of the population and comprised 75% of the entire population of 19.5 million in 2001. Although Colombo is relatively small it is the major commercial and administrative centre of Sri Lanka. The total residential population of the city was 642,020 in 2001 (Sinhalese 40.9%; Sri Lankan Tamils 29.7%; Indian Tamils 2.2%; Muslims 23.6%; and Others 3.6%); the daily floating population of Colombo has been estimated to be around 400,000 people. Colombo remains a city of diversity and complexity, constrained by the physical limitations of sea, harbour, lakes and rivers. A rich ethnic mix consisting primarily of Sinhala, Ceylon Tamils, and Muslims (Ceylon Moors) populate this low-lying port city, many of them live in slums (22,358) and in shanty settlements (20,685).

This present empirical study on urban, low-income[10] neighbourhoods focussed on areas affected by the 1983 riots. There is information to prove that, with exception the Tamils living in slum neighbourhoods, a significant number of Tamils in Colombo were also harassed by mobs in July 1983. As a result of this and other related ethnic factors serious bomb blasts and similar major attacks, have occurred in the city. These events have made life tense and stressful for various social classes among the residents of the city. In relation to this, the study also focused on the way in which slum dwellers live together despite ethnic differences in their neighbourhoods. Thus, the main objective of this sociological study was to understand the "ethnic differences and urban neighbourhood relationships among the slum dwellers in the context of Colombo city." It also has four related sub-objectives: (1) To understand the socio-economic profile of the slum dwellers under focus; (2) To find

---

[10] Low-Income: According to the United Nations Development Program (UNDP), income poverty refers to the percentage of the population living on less than US$ 1 a day.

out the physical[11] and social[12] boundaries of neighbourhood relationships among the slum dwellers; (3) To identify individual and community level social networks[13] of the slum dwellers; and (4) To
understand neighbourhood sentiments and inter-community harmony.

The study is exploratory in nature. It focused on two selected
slum neighbourhoods in Colombo city. The Random sampling
method was used to select the sample for the study. The sample size
was kept at 200 units (respondents-households) from both the
neighbourhoods. It formed about 10 percent of the total number of
households. Thus, out of 706 households in Kirulapura (A)
neighbourhood 100 units were selected and out of 703 households in
Magazine Road (B) 100 units were selected. Kirulapura and Magazine Road are situated in the Colombo Municipal Council (CMC)
area. Kirulapura[14] is a heterogeneous neighbourhood, where Sinhalese, Tamils, Muslims, Burghers, and Malayalees live together.
Magazine Road[15] is a homogeneous neighbourhood, where majority
of the people are Sinhalese. Thus, the study was a comparison between heterogeneous Kirulapura (Sinhalese 44%; Sri Lankan Tamils
34%; Indian Tamils 2%; Muslims 18%; Burgher 1%; and Malayalee
1%), and the more homogeneous Magazine Road (Sinhalese 89%;
Sri Lankan Tamils 7%; Muslims 2%; and Burgher 2%) neighbour-

---

[11] Physical boundaries may be material (eg: roads, railways, rivers, parks, lines etc) or
symbolic (eg: block numbers) and may reinforce each other and may be marked off
in some distinctive and recognizable manner, and therefore has a ecological relation
to the rest of the community.

[12] Social boundaries: Within its physical boundaries, a neighbourhood contains inhabitants having something in common, which gives them a certain collective character. The sociological conception of neighbourhood emphasizes the notion of shared
activities, experiences (use of area facilities for shopping. leisure etc.) and values; a
sociological conception best realized in certain social cultural enclaves within a larger
urban area.

[13] Social network: Individual or more rarely collectives who are linked together by
one or more social relationships, thus forming a social network (eg: relatives, friendships, neighbours, co-workers etc.).

[14] The Kirulapura slum neighbourhood (mixed slum and shanties) is situated in the
Parmamkada East Ward (no. 45) of the CMC, two minutes walk from the Kirula-
pone Town.

[15] The Magazine Road slum neighbourhood is situated three minutes walk from the
Borella town in the Borella North Ward (no. 33) of the CMC.

hoods. Total number of persons of the sample population in Kiru-lapura was 540, and in Magazine Road 544.

The present study has been based on quantitative and quali-tative methods, using a custom-designed survey. The three main re-search tools employed for data collection consisted of a sample survey – using an interview schedule, in-depth interviews (informal interviews) and participant observation in a limited way. The sample survey included questions on respondents' socio-demographic char-acteristics – such as sex, age, marital status, religion, ethnicity, caste, education, language skills, number of adults, children, school-going children, youth, and earners living in the household; occupation, in-come, expenditure, ownership of household materials etc. Further, there were also questions on migration and settlements, neighbour-hood relationships (with relatives, friends, neighbours), ethnic rela-tionships, work relationships, political relationships, cultural activities, leisure activities, membership in associations and related activities, external social relationships, attitude regarding security, satisfaction with the neighbourhood, and sense of community.

Data for this study, both quantitative and qualitative, were collected within a three-month time period (29th March 2002 to 30th June 2002). The study took place in 2002. The "interview schedule" included 20 pages and contained 98 questions and 17 statements. There were 96 structured (short) questions and 19 open-ended ques-tions. It took an average of 60 minutes to complete an "interview schedule." In-depth interview took half an hour more. The researcher used participant observation as a tool in a limited way especially at evenings and week ends too (Saturdays and Sundays). A minimum of three households were interviewed per day while the maximum num-ber was four. Both males (89 - 44.5%) and females 111 - (55.5%) were represented in the sample.

The researcher analysed the data by using simple frequency tables and cross tabulation was made for showing relationship be-tween important variables. Further, the processed data was analysed by using the three statistical measures on 'neighbourhood,' Wallin's Women Neighbourliness Scale, Bogardus's Social Distance Scale, and Buckner's Sub-Scales of Neighbourhood Cohesion Scale. However, the sample of this study is neither large nor representative enough to allow for generalisations about the city of Colombo, leave alone cities in general but it is believed that the findings relating to the particular neighbourhoods under consideration will provide valuable guidelines to more exhaustive and comprehensive research. Further, the researcher firmly hopes the findings reported here will help for both future urban research as well as urban policy.

II: MAIN FINDINGS

The following pages contain the research findings that emerged out of the present study. The researcher found that the two neighbourhoods have existed for more than 50 years. Out of the 100 heads of households, 84% in Kirulapura and 91% in Magazine Road have full residential ownership. Furthermore, it was found that migration shows interesting patterns in both neighbourhoods. Out of the 100 heads of households, 70% in Kirulapura and 67% in Magazine Road have urban backgrounds and had migrated to their current residences from various regions. It was also found that the 36% of the households in Kirulapura and 27% in Magazine Road migrated from the Colombo Metropolitan Area. Further, around 10% of the people in both the neighbourhoods are migrants from suburban and semi-urban areas. The remaining 20% of people migrated from various rural areas of Sri Lanka. The reasons for migration were the hope of finding a better job, marriage, displacement (due to public and private intervention), and also the ethnic conflict.

The overall picture emerging out of this comparative analysis suggests that the two selected neighbourhoods are fairly comparable to each other in terms of migration, tenure of accommodation, total number of population, sex ratio, age groupings, marital status, structure of the household members (e.g. adults, youths, earners), and types of family. Differences, however, emerged when factors such as religious composition, ethnic composition, caste, education levels, language skills, occupational structure, monthly household income, expenditure, and consumer patterns of the slum dwellers' are taken into consideration. The analysis of the data on education, income and occupation, the three main determinants of socio-economic status (SES), leads the researcher to conclude that Magazine Road neighbourhood has a higher socio-economic status than the Kirulapura neighbourhood.

In both neighbourhoods, kinship ties are closely linked to social life of the residents. On the one hand, it should be noted that kinship relationships seem to be more powerful in case of Magazine Road. On other hand, evidence of a 51% rate inter-ethnic marriage in the heterogeneous neighbourhood of Kirulapura reveals valuable trends regarding mixed inter-ethnic or kinship networks. It was found that along with internal kinship networks, residents also have strong external kinship relations in other slum neighbourhoods in the Colombo Metropolitan Area, which indicates the presence of community level kinship and ethnic ties in the city.

Further, the researcher found that the heterogeneous slum neighbourhood exhibited different types of social relationships in comparison to the homogeneous neighbourhood. Thus, friend and neighbour relationship ties are displayed at a higher level in the Kirulapura. However, crimes and crime-related activities played a major role in Magazine Road, which basically increased fear among the residents and restricted their social relationships to their families or kinship networks. As a result, day-to-day life and other important social relationships like friendships, neighbourliness, have weakened in Magazine Road.

As expected, participation in community development activities and festivals was found to be higher, and attitudes towards philanthropy better during difficult times, in the homogeneous neighbourhood rather than in the heterogeneous one. This may be due to the fact that community level activities are beneficial to all inhabitants in the homogeneous neighbourhood. Participation in special occasions like weddings, puberty celebrations or birthday's parties, may give personal satisfaction and also cannot be avoided, if within the neighbourhood. However, engagement in leisure activities among people in Magazine Road was recorded at a higher level than at Kirulapura. Low participation in leisure activities in Kirulapura also indicates that the inhabitants were engaged in daily work to improve the economic status of their households. Also, low participation in formal associations in homogeneous neighbourhood can be contrasted with somewhat higher levels of participation displayed in the heterogeneous neighbourhood. Kirulapura is a re-developed neighbourhood and formal associations set up in the area have been helpful to the residents. However, various political ideologies among

inhabitants in Magazine Road seem to have led to their low participation in associations there.

When faced with sudden illness, majority of inhabitants in
both neighbourhoods approached the government or private hospi-
tals. But, many have also approached their neighbours. In case of
family problems, the majority attempted an internal solution, while
some also approached their relatives. In case of any legal problems
residents of both slums contacted the nearest police officer. If there
were any administrative problems, people of both neighbourhoods
contacted the Colombo Municipal Council or various politicians.
Also, the Community Development Centre in Kirulapura helps people in the community. Comparatively, Magazine Road people depend
more on external organisations.

It is very clear that both neighbourhoods have witnessed
various interventions from the government during their settlement
procedure. The United National Party [UNP] government re-
developed Kirulapura and the residents benefited from this project.
Therefore, most of the community members support the UNP and
this has led to the political hegemony of UNP in the slum. This has
also helped to keep Kirulapura politically peaceful as no other political party could challenge UNP. But, the situation is completely different in Magazine Road. This slum garden, despite having a higher
economic status than that of Kirulapura, has not been re-developed.
Four political parties are active there. The major political parties –
UNP and Sri Lanka Freedom Party [SLFP] – are very competitive
with each other in Magazine Road, the result being that no one party
has political hegemony in the neighbourhood. Other major feature is
the presence of two Marxist radical political parties – the Janatha
Vimukthi Peramuna [JVP] and the Lanka Sama Samaja Pakshaya
[LSSP]. This has provided for a more competitive political background. Thus, in the same slum neighbourhood people are divided
according to their political ideologies and this has led to displeasure
and disintegrated environment among the residents. Various regimes,
from time-to-time, have settled their supports in this slum, and this
has structured the political ideologies of residents. Thus, political
participation in Magazine Road was higher than in the Kirulapura
neighbourhood, but frequent elections in the country have weakened
relations among neighbours and disturbed social harmony.

An important finding is the positive attitude towards inter-ethnic marriages and neighbour relations. We have seen that 51% of the residents of Kirulapura and 25% of Magazine Road practiced inter-ethnic marriages. Using the Bogardus's "Social Distance Scale" the researcher had asked each community respectively, "Do you mind close kinship relations by marriage with Sinhalese/Tamil/Muslim/Burgher/Malayees?" The overall picture of the responses can be summarised as follows: In Kirulapura, almost half of Sinhalese were open to the idea of marrying into any other ethnic group. Also, significantly, 72% of Tamils were willing to marry other ethnic groups. The most significant finding is that 82% of Tamils were more willing to marry a Sinhalese than any other ethnic groups. However, only half of the Sinhalese was willing to marry a Tamil. Among the Muslims 33% of them stated they were willing to marry into other ethnic communities but 67% of Muslims are opposed to such an idea. The Muslim community also put forward a condition that anybody from other ethnic group marrying into their community would have to convert to Islam. Overall as many as 68% of the minorities were willing to marry a Sinhalese. Comparatively, in the Magazine Road neighbourhood only 30% of residents were willing to marry into other ethnic communities. In contrast, 73% of the minorities in Magazine Road were willing to marry the majority Sinhalese. Despite communal polarisation in society, non-Sinhalese households are receptive to high integration with the majority community.

Other major positive thinking on neighbour relations was that residents of both neighbourhoods stated that they did not have problems with persons of other ethnic groups associating with them, as personal friends, and, in general as citizens of the country.

As mentioned earlier, Kirulapura is an ethnically balanced community. Therefore, 78% of the residents can speak Sinhala as well as Tamil. This has proved to be an advantage to residents, when expressing their own views about other community members and also in understanding each other's needs, attitudes, values, norms, patterns of life and problems. This has led to an understanding that all people are human and similar. In such situations, ethnic differences are not antagonistic. Thus, the north-south divide of the country, on ethnic lines, is hardly visible among the communities under focus.

The researcher could not find any discrimination against any ethnic group in the neighbourhood. A miscreant or a wrongdoer is punished without any consideration to his ethnic background, whether Sinhala, Tamil or Muslim. The residents were more concerned about their economic condition than their ethnic background. They had even protected their Tamil relatives, friends, and neighbours from the mobs during the 1983 riot. Some of the Tamils (elder citizens) living in the neighbourhood were not happy with the Sinhalese-biased social transformation carried out by S.W.R.D. Bandaranaike in 1956. They found that "The Sinhala Only" Official Act of 1956 gave rise to feelings of frustration and isolation among the Tamils and leading to their belief that the Sinhala government was discriminating against the Tamils.

The social and political environment in Magazine Road was quite different from Kirulapura: the community was divided by various political ideologies. Another major finding was the existence of a negative relationship between neighbours due to political unrest and the fear of crime in the Magazine Road. Living in a neighbourhood environment that is perceived as dangerous leads to more distanced social relationships among neighbours. The ethnic groups did not differ much in the degree of dangerous environments they faced but, regardless of ethnic background, fear of crime has led to a reduction in the number of locally based social relationships, in Magazine Road.

It is difficult to analyse the situation as a whole without adequate (in-depth) details of the experiences of some of the residents in both neighbourhoods during 1983 riot. The violence began on ethnic lines and was directed against Tamils. Some groups of Sinhalese, a few Sinhala political parties and trade unions were involved in the violence. Business and trade rivalries also fuelled the violence. Many Tamil businessmen and their networks, in the city centre, were targeted. There is also evidence that some Tamils killed each other due to rivalry arising out of property, money or jealousy.

People of both slums displayed their political awareness of the ethnic social strife in the country. More than 85% of residents in both neighbourhoods stated that "discussion" was the main solution for ethnic conflict. On the other hand, around 10% of them stated that either "war" or "discussion" could be a solution but it should be undertaken honestly. According to their own views, this meant: "Do not think of taking any political or economic advantages from this problem. This is our country's problem, we should solve the problem together, honesty."

Further, the study found that residents of both the neighbourhoods had reasons for satisfaction and dissatisfaction. Thus, 42% of Kirulapura respondents and 28% in Magazine Road were satisfied with the friendly attitude of their neighbours. Another reason identified as contributing to neighbourhood satisfaction was the 'helpful attitude' of the people, which was reported by 25% of the residents in Kirulapura and by 35% in Magazine Road. 'Being of the same status' was also identified as a reason for satisfaction among 15% of the people in Kirulapura and 11% in Magazine Road.

On the other hand, residents of both neighbourhoods were dissatisfied with their neighbours for being 'noisy' (43% in Kirulapura and 33% in Magazine Road). Especially Magazine Road residents were dissatisfied with their neighbours for 'interfering' (26%), 'drug business' (11%), and 'homicide' (10%), respectively. However, 40% of the people in Kirulapura stated that they were satisfied with their neighbourhood.

Kirulapura residents and 79% of residents in Magazine Road said that they felt secure living in the neighbourhood. Thus, 67 residents (73%) in Kirulapura and 31 residents (38%) in Magazine Road felt secure because of their neighbours' 'faithfulness.' Another significant reason identified was the availability of various facilities in the Colombo city, which was mentioned by 44 residents (54%) in Magazine Road. On the other hand, nine residents (100%) in Kirulapura stated that they felt insecure in the neighbourhood because of drug addicts and drug-related thieves. Out of 21 residents, 11 (52%) in Magazine Road said that they were insecure due to large-scale drug businesses; also 10 people (47%) felt insecure because of sudden killings in the neighbourhood.

Another important finding was that majority of people in Kirulapura were willing to continue living in the same neighbourhood while 63% in Magazine Road 63% were unwilling to do so. Accordingly, majority of the people in Kirulapura and Magazine Road were willing to move from their present neighbourhoods.

However, 16% in Kirulapura rated their neighbourhood as a "good" place to live in, while 73% rated it as "fairly good." Comparatively, in Magazine Road 64% rated their neighbourhood as "fairly good," and 27% rated it as "fairly poor." Thus, desired mobility could be for better housing and social status.

The "neighbourhood cohesion scale" was used to measure social cohesion among the people. Some 17 'statements' relevant were found to the three neighbourhood sub-scales on "attraction to neighbourhood," "neighbourliness," and "psychological sense of neighbourhood." Under the sub scale – "attraction to neighbour-hood" three statements were tested. 83% of the residents in Kiru-lapura stated that they were attracted to their neighbourhood, while 66% said so in Magazine Road. Also, 67% of the people in Kiru-lapura felt like moving out of the neighbourhood, while 86% among the respondents in Magazine Road also wanted to move out of their neighbourhood. However, 84% of the people in Kirulapura said that they would prefer to continue residing in their neighbourhood. Also, 75% of the people in Magazine Road wanted to go on living in the neighbourhood. Thus, overall "attraction to the neighbourhood" is better in Kirulapura (Mean = 8.1600) than Magazine Road (Mean = 7.2600).

Regarding "neighbourliness" six statements were tested. According to the scale, in Kirulapura 80% visit their neighbours' homes. Comparatively, in Magazine Road 60% do so. Further, when in need of advice, 77% of Kirulapura residents and 56% of Magazine Road residents approached their neighbours. Another important finding is that almost all the people in Kirulapura and Magazine Road believe that in an emergency their neighbours would help them. While, on the one hand, 68% of the people in Kirulapura borrowed and exchanged things with their neighbours, in Magazine Road 65% didn't do so. On the other hand, 52% in Kirulapura agreed with the statement "Neighbours rarely visit my house." 61% in Magazine Road agreed with this statement. While 69% in Kiru-lapura regularly stopped to talk with their neighbours, only 37% people in Magazine Road practiced this. Comparatively, the feeling of "neighbourliness" was also higher in Kirulapura (Mean = 16.7300) than Magazine Road (Mean = 14.7600).

Regarding the "psychological sense of neighbourhood," eight statements were tested. It was observed that 87% in Kirulapura and 85% in Magazine Road felt they belonged to the neighbourhood. Further, 86% in Kirulapura valued friendships and associations they had formed with other people in their neighbourhood while 76% in Magazine Road felt similarly. In addition, almost all the people in Kirulapura and Magazine Road agreed with the statement that, "if the people in their neighbourhood were planning something, it meant that 'we' were doing it rather than 'they' were doing."

Likewise, 91% in Kirulapura and 82% in Magazine Road felt that they were loyal to their neighbours. An important fact identified was that almost all the people in both the neighbourhoods were willing to work together to improve their neighbourhoods. While, 60% in Kirulapura felt they had a lot in common with their neighbours but 63% in Magazine Road felt differently. Almost all the residents of Kirulapura thought that living in the neighbourhood gave them a "sense of community." A lesser proportion (77%) of the people in Magazine Road felt similarly. Thus, "psychological sense of neighbourhood" was better in Kirulapura (Mean = 22.8500) than in Magazine Road (Mean = 21.3200). Comparatively, the study reveals that Kirulapura neighbourhood was better than Magazine Road in all three aspects of social cohesion.

III: DISCUSSION

About the economic condition of the urban poor in Colombo city in early 1980, Newton Gunasinghe remarked:

> Of crucial importance is the accelerated process of internal social differentiation among the urban poor that sets in with the opening up of the economy. The urban poor, which consisted of certain layers of working class, the *lumpen* proletariat, itinerant workers, vendors and carters, which in the earlier period suffered an equality of poverty, were subject to a process of internal economic differentiation, as economic opportunities expanded. The mass exodus to West Asia from the ranks of the urban poor strengthened the economic position of these households from which the migrant workers

emerged, as a substantial proportion of their income was re-patriated to the country.[16]

Additionally, as Hewamanne and Brow have argued:

The female roles defined and projected in this [pre-1977] ideology – which idealised women as full-time housewives, mothers and homemakers – were seriously challenged after 1977, when a new program of economic liberalisation re-placed the previous socialist State- controlled economic poli-cies. The United National Party (UNP), which came to power at this time, vigorously promoted free-market policies and thereby opened the economy to foreign investment.[17]

As a result of this process of structural adjustment in the economic policy, the last two decades witnessed significant socio-economic, and cultural changes in Sri Lanka.

The researcher concours with the above analysis of Newton Gunasinghe for that period, but further additions should be made to those observations in the current context, after 25 years of the open economic system in Sri Lanka. There has been a strong connection between open economy and the ethnic problem in Sri Lanka. For ex-ample, Tamil farmers in the Northeast were disappointed by the ef-fects of economic liberalisation because their main agricultural products like onion, chilli, and tobacco had lesser demand in a com-petitive market economy.

Since 1980, a large number of Tamil refugees, who were dis-placed by war, migrated to Colombo city. Some of them migrated to Western countries and even to Tamil Nadu (India). According to An-ton Balasingham, "More than 800,000 people, mostly Tamils, were displaced by war."[18] As a result, North-East Tamils and Muslims were permanently or temporarily settled in Colombo city. Thus, the environment provided good opportunities to three-wheeler driv-

---

[16] Newton Gunasinghe, "The Open Economy & Its Impact on Ethnic Relations in Sri Lanka," in Lanka Guardian, Vol. 6, No. 17, January 1, 1984: 6-8+15; Vol. 6, No. 18, January 15, 1984: 15-17, 1 table; Vol. 6, No. 19, February 1, 1984: 10-12.

[17] Sandya Hewamanne, and James Brow, "If they Allow Us We will Fight," in *Consciousness Among Women Workers in the Katunayake Free Trade Zone*. The Society for the Anthropology of Work, unit of the American Anthropological Association. Vol. xix, No. 3, (1999).

ers/owners. In the wake of these migrations, the majority of three wheeler drivers residing in Colombo slum areas made a good income, through various legal and illegal means. Some drivers stated that their net income was SLRs: 30,000 to 40,000 per month. According to Chamath Ariyadasa, about a million people were displaced by the war, with about 400,000 believed to have returned home since February 2002,[19] after the comencement of the peace process, much to the disappointment of the three-wheel drivers, whoes incomes were considerably reduced, after this.

Another major result of the open economy and the war was the emergence of large-scale drug businesses. Significant number of Tamils, Muslims and a few Sinhalese were engaged in drug pedalling leading to the rise in the number of drug addicts among youth. According to the National Dangerous Drugs Control Board (NDDCB) 15,120 drug-related arrests were made in 2002. A survey has been conducted among the low-income settlements in the city by the Public Health Department of the CMC in collaboration with NDDCB in 2001, which identified 2,356 heroin addicts. According to the views of both the organisations, actual number of heroin addicts in the city may be more than 20,000.[20] Therefore, drug addiction and drug business can be considered a serious social problem among urban slums dwellers in Colombo city.

As a result of the open economic system and ethnic social strife, a new social phenomenon emerged whereby slum dwellers were directly or indirectly exposed to opportunities of making money and used some portion of it to sustain themselves. While formerly owning of luxury goods was a distant dream, currently overt display of such goods in both slum neighbourhoods is regarded as normal.

Thus, the open economic system and ethnic strife in Sri Lanka has had both a positive and negative effect on the slum dwellers. Under these new economic circumstances, a significant number

---

[18] *The Times of India*, May 1, 2003.
[19] Chamath Ariyadasa "Lankan Rebels Cook Up a Mean Landmine," *The Indian Express*, June 3, 2003).
[20] *Poverty Profile, City of Colombo: Urban Poverty Reduction Through Community Empowerment*, (Colombo: Colombo Municipal Council, 2002), 26.

of slum dwellers rose to lower middle-class or even middle class level. However, majority of them still remain at the lower class level. Also, there is evidence that after achieving a better economic condition, some of the residents left the slums and settled in semi-urban areas (e.g. Homagama, Padukka, Hokandara).

As noted earlier, there are two major views on slum communities, in the litrature: the 'anti-social'[21] and the 'social cohesion'[22] view. How far are these two views relevant to the Kirulapura and Magazine Road neighbourhoods? How far are such processes relevant to the Kirulapura and Magazine Road neighbourhoods? Are they organized or disorganized? As we discussed so far, the findings relevant to the Kirulapura showed that this heterogeneous neighbourhood is well organized. Note that most of the literature on the West has shown that heterogeneous neighbourhoods would have more crime, and be socially disorganized. However, the slum is not only a place where people live; it is also a place of mutual understanding and intimate social relationships. With regard to Magazine Road, since there is a competitive political environment, and some criminal activities, this may lead to the might the conclusion that this homogeneous neighbourhood is disorganised. But, the researcher does not endorse such a view. In a similar study, Anderson and Mary Pattillo McCoy[23] discussed the role of drug dealers, gang members, and other street criminals in exerting social control over other com-

---

[21] H. W. Zorbaugh, *Gold Coast and the Slum* (Chicago: The University of Chicago Press, 1957); N.P. Gist and L.A. Halbert, *Urban Society* (New York: Thomas Y. Crowell and Company, 1950); M.B. Clinard, *Slums and Community Development: Experiment in Self-Help* (New York: Free Press, 1966); P.P. Karan, W.A. Bladen & G. Singh, "Sum Dwellers and Squatters Images of the City," in *Environment and Behaviour.* Vol. 12, No. 1. (March 1980), 81-100; R.B. Mandal, *Urban Geography. A Textbook.* (New Delhi: Concept Publishing Company, 2000).

[22] Bruce Kapferer, *Shanty Town in Developing Nations,* (New York: Wenner Gren Foundation for Anthropological Research, July, 1977); T.K. Majumdar, The Urban poor and Social Change in *A Study of Squatter Settlements in Delhi, eds.,* by Alfred de Souza (New Delhi: Manohar Publications, 1978); N. Ratna Rao, Social Organization in An Indian Slum in *Study of a Caste Slum* (New Delhi: Mittal Publications, 1990); Kalinga Tudor Silva and Karunatissa Athukorale, *The Watta Dwellers: A Sociological Study of Selected Urban low-Income Communities in Sri Lanka* (Lanham: University Press of America, 1991); Arachchige-Don S. Naville, *Patterns of Community Structure in Colombo, Sri Lanka* (Lanham: University Press of America, 1994); Vandana Desai, *Community Participation and Slum Housing: A Study of Bombay* (New Delhi: Sage Publications. 1995).

[23] Cited in Body-Gendrot, *op. cit.*, 2000.

munity residents in either conventional or deviant ways. The situation, discussed by Anderson and McCoy, is very similar with Magazine Road. Few residents are involved with gangs that controlling Magazine Road neighbourhood. Hence, majority of Magazine Road residents were dissatisfied with their environment and even ready to move from the neighbourhood.

Manuel Castells revealed that the permanent and ever extending intervention of the State apparatus in area of processes and units of consumption, makes it the real source of order in everyday life.[24] This intervention of the State apparatus, which we call urban planning in the broad sense, involves an almost immediate politicisation of the whole urban problematic. Peter Saunders[25] explained that the result is a crisis in the provision of collective consumption. The basic problems – lack of housing, poor health care, inadequate schooling, poor transportation facilities, shortage of cultural amenities and so on – that led the State to intervene in the process of consumption thus reappear. What is different, however, is that the whole area of consumption has now become politicised; the more the State assumes responsibility for the provision of social resources, the more centrally involved it becomes in the organisation of everyday life and the more everyday life is politicised as a result. As mentioned by these leading urban sociologists, the Kirulapura and Magazine Road neighbourhoods also have been politicised due to the interventions from time to time by various political parties.

As mentioned, Kirulapura is an ethnically balanced community. Over three-fourths of the residents speak Sinhala and Tamil. Gore mentioned, "In a multi-lingual neighbourhood it is not only the mother tongue that is important, but also the ability to speak languages other than one's own. The fewer languages one knows, more restricted the number of linguistic groups in which one can function effectively. When a person knows more than one language he/she increases not only his/her own chances of communicating with others, but also the chance of others sections to communicate with

---

[24] Manuel Castells, *The Urban Question*. (London: Edward Arnold Publishers Ltd, 1977)
[25] Peter Saunders, *The Theory and the Urban Question*. (London: Hutchinson & co. Publishers Limited, 1981).

him/her."[26] Gananath Obeyesekere[27] explained "The Sinhalese speak an Indo-European language (Sinhala) while the Tamils speak a Dravidian one. Underlying language and religious difference, Buddhist versus Hindu, are strong cultural and racial similarities. Physically the two groups cannot be differentiated." As we have seen in the heterogeneous neighbourhood of Kirulapura, a majority of people can speak Sinhala and Tamil. Despite religious differences, Muslims can speak Tamil as well as Sinhala. This is an important social fact to consider, when settling people on the basis of ethnic backgrounds in planned neighbourhood housing units, for it can enhance ethnic harmony.

Thus, the overall data suggests that neighbourhood life has a variety of dimensions. Different features of neighbourhood – personal, physical, geographical, and institutional – offer strong incentives for involvement and as a result community feelings will be high. When neighbourhoods provide disincentives for involvement to their residents, the sense of community is low. Therefore, the neighbourhood, and not just the residents, plays an important role in constructing a community. Community can be strong in neighbourhoods where residents have extensive external ties if it encourages involvement, and it can be weak in where residents have few external ties if it discourages involvement. The services provided by the neighbourhood, characteristics of the residents, and social and emotional ties within the neighbourhood are factors, which influences what people feel about their neighbourhood. It is a combination of all of these factors that determine the strength of communal bonds within neighbourhood.

Ahlbrandt[28] mentions that people's behaviour is constrained by their socio-economic circumstances and also by the characteristics of neighbourhood in which they live. The neighbourhood environment, through the quality of life it offers, availability of services, and fabric of its social life, influences peoples' decisions about participat-

---

[26] Gore, *op.cit.*, 215.
[27] Gananath Obeyesekere, "Political Violence and the Future of Democracy in Sri Lanka," in *The Toronto Lanka Review*, (March April, 1984), 3-23 & and also in *Sri Lanka: The Ethnic Conflict, Perspectives, Myths, and realities*, (ed.) Committee for Rational Development, (New Delhi: Navrang Publishers), 70-94.

ing in neighbourhood activities. People living in a neighbourhood that offers a variety of services – religious, recreational, outings, and day-to-day activities – have a greater choice about utilising these services. People living in a neighbourhood with a strong social fabric – a place in which significant interpersonal interaction occurs – have more opportunities to meet their social and emotional needs than those living in neighbourhoods where social fabric is weak or non-existent. Thus, those living in a neighbourhood in which quality of life are desirable, as evidenced by a low crime rate and safe streets, have a greater incentive to go out and participate in neighbourhood activities than those living in places where fear of crime keeps people housebound.

These characteristics of the neighbourhood environment may also reinforce one another in constructing a stronger or weaker community. For instance, a neighbourhood that has many local services increases the opportunities for its residents to interact, and this may lead to a stronger social fabric. Or, a neighbourhood with a high crime rate may discourage people from maintaining neighbourhood connections and as a result fabric of its social life will be weak.

The above findings have some implications for theoretical perspectives on urban neighbourhoods. Three different theoretical approaches have been suggested in the study of differences in local neighbourhood relationships: (1) compression theory, (2) avoidance theory, and (3) compositional perspective. The compositional perspective emphasises that ethnic groups might differ in a variety of characteristics that affect neighbourliness. Herbert Gans argued that social class rather than ethnic identity has a decisive effect on locally based informal relationships.[29] If members of one ethnic group are more residentially stable or more likely to own their homes than members of another group, then these social investments and not ethnicity *per se* may account for variation in neighbour relationships. Thus, according to this perspective, apparent ethnic differences should disappear after other attributes, such as socio-economic status, home-ownership and family status. In other words, composi-

---

[28] Roger S. Ahlbrandt Jr., *Neighbouroods, People, and Community*, (New York: Plenum Publishing Corporation, 1984).
[29] J. Herbert Gans, *The Urban Villagers: Group and Class in Life of Italian-Americans*. (New York: The Free Press of Glencoe, 1962).

tional perspective argues that ethnic differences in locally based social ties are spurious, resulting from other differences such as socio-
economic status and life cycle stage. Findings of the present study in
the case of Kirulapura fully support this compositional perspective. It
was observed that despite the ethnic differences in Kirulapura
neighbourhood, its residents were more concerned about their socio-
economic activities and neighbourhood relationships.

Barry Wellman and Barry Leighton[30] have succinctly discussed some of these issues and proposed three forms of community
that may continue to exist in contemporary metropolitan society: (1)
the lost community in which individuals have few social ties at the
local (such a neighbourhood) or extra-local level, (2) the saved community in which individuals primarily relate to others in their immediate neighbourhoods, and (3) the liberated community in which
individuals have primarily non-neighbourhood social ties. Although,
Wellman and Leighton did not take a strong stand on the importance
of each type of community, they seemed to believe that the most
likely form of community is the "liberated" community in which local ties have declined, whereas non-local ties persist or even increase.

Scholars of the 'saved community tradition' have tended to
regard human beings as fundamentally good and inherently gregari-
ous. They are viewed as apt to organise self-regulating communities
under all circumstances, even extreme conditions of poverty, oppression, or catastrophe. The neighbourhood unit has been the 20th century planning ideal for new housing. Saved ideologues have also
argued for the necessity to preserve existing neighbourhoods against
the predations of ignorant and rapacious institutions. The saved argument has been the ideological foundation of neighbourhood
movement, which seeks to stop expressways, demolish developers,
and renovate old areas. The liberated argument is fundamentally op-
timistic about urban life. It is appreciative of urban diversity; imputa-
tions of social disorganization and pathology find little place within
it. The liberated argument has had an important impact on thinking
about political phenomena, especially that related to collective disor-
ders.

The findings of this sociological study have implications for models of social neighbourhood. Observations on the Kirulapura neighbourhood support notion of the 'saved community,' which argues that individuals primarily relate to others in their immediate neighbourhoods. Findings from Magazine Road partially support the notion of the 'liberated community,' which argues that social changes have increased the geographical mobility of individuals and has therefore 'liberated' the community from the constraints of place. However, the liberated argument agrees with the saved argument's contention that primary ties have remained viable, useful, and important. It shares the saved argument's contention that communities still flourish in the city, but it maintains that such communities are rarely organised within neighbourhoods. After introducing the open economic system, drug market networks and related crimes have led to tension and fear among the residents in Magazine Road. It has resulted in low-level relationships among them, and led to dependence on the external relationships. Overall, the two slum neighbourhoods in Colombo city under present focus emerge as diversified neighbourhoods in terms of social cohesion, neighbourly relations and ethnic relationships. There are several positive forces bringing social cohesion than disruptive forces (like crime and political manoeuvres) affecting friendly environment in the settlements under present focus.

The positive forms of social cohesion that identified in the Kirulapura location will help others to understand why these forms did not appear in the in the areas of violent and conflict in other part of the country. The lessons learnt from this study can be applied even to develop a national social integration among different ethnic community in the country.

Niriellage Chandrasiri Niriella *is a Senior Lecturer in Sociology and Urban Studies at the University of Colombo, Sri Lanka. He obtained his M.Phil. in Social Sciences (Urban Studies) from the TATA Institute of Social Sciences (TISS), Mumbai, India.*

---

[30] Barry Wellman and Barry Leighton, "Networks, Neighbourhoods, and Communities" in *Approaches to the Study of the Community Question*, Ronald L. Warren and Larry Lyon (ed.) (Illinois: The Dorsey Press, 1983), 246 - 262.

Towards a political economy of Sri Lanka's 'ethnic' conflict

Dhananjayan Sriskandarajah

ABSTRACT:

Despite a growing literature on the economics of political conflict, relatively little attention has been paid to how politico-economic factors have shaped conflict in Sri Lanka. Inspired by the work of the late Newtown Gunasinghe, this article seeks to highlight the heuristic potential of political economy for the study of Sri Lanka's 'ethnic' conflict. Three particular questions are explored: why did hostilities occur when they did, why has the conflict lasted so long and why has there been a move towards peace lately? The article suggests that economic mechanisms, structures, and powers have been at the heart of ethno-political mobilisation. The article maps Sri Lanka's 'war economy' in which the two main protagonists (and the economy as a whole) were able to mobilize the required financial resources to wage war; in which the adverse economic impacts on key stakeholders were minimized so as not to consolidate opposition to war; and in which key stakeholders derived economic benefits. Finally, the article explores how economic factors may have induced the Sri Lankan government and the Liberation Tigers of Tamil Eelam (LTTE) to sign a ceasefire in 2002. It is suggested that understanding the linkages between material conditions and political crises is critical not only to the historiography of Sri Lanka's conflict but also to understanding what levers might be deployed to further peace in the future in Sri Lanka and perhaps elsewhere.

PROLOGUE

In 1984, the late Newton Gunasinghe published a landmark essay on 'The Open Economy & Its Impact on Ethnic Relations in Sri Lanka.'[1] Though short, written for a general audience and con-

---

[1] The essay was originally published in *Lanka Guardian* in three parts: 6, no.17, 7 January 1984, 6-15; 6, no.18, 14 January 1984, 15-18; 6,19, 21 January 1984, 10-12. Since then, it has been reproduced in several books, including in *Sri Lanka, The Ethnic Conflict: Myths, Realities and Perspectives*, ed., Committee for Rational Development (New Delhi: Narvang, 1984); *Facets of Ethnicity in Sri Lanka*, eds.,

taining only a handful of concrete examples, the essay is nevertheless a significant contribution to scholarship on Sri Lanka's political economy and its ethnic relations. Described as 'controversial'[2] and 'brilliant,'[3] the essay has been hailed as 'easily the most thoughtful and fluent attempt to link economic liberalisation to the ethnic conflict.'[4] Gunasinghe's work, especially its central aim of exposing the economic contradictions that lie beneath, what is often seen as the 'ethnic' conflict, has been a major influence on this author's own approach. Two decades on, this article revisits Gunasinghe's main concerns, and attempts to develop some of his insights.

INTRODUCTION

Sri Lanka's 'ethnic' conflict – variously labelled as civil war, communal strife, guerrilla insurgency, terrorist threat, the Tamil 'question,' the 'national' problem or, simply, 'the troubles' – has been a prominent feature of Sri Lanka's social, political, and economic landscape for more than two decades. Although ostensibly built upon competition and antagonism between Sri Lanka's two main ethnic groups, the Sinhalese and the Tamils, the conflict is not simply the 'twentieth century manifestation of an age-old rivalry between two peoples.'[5] Instead, as elsewhere, the ethno-political conflict in Sri Lanka is contingent, contextual, dynamic, strategic and often rational in nature.

In recent years, there has been a growing interest amongst researchers and policy makers in the economic factors that might ex-

---

Charles Abeysekera and Newton Gunasinghe (Colombo: Social Scientists Association, 1984); *Newton Gunasinghe: Selected Essays,* ed., Sasanka Perera (Colombo: Social Scientists Association, 1996); and *Economy, Culture And Civil War In Sri Lanka,* eds., Deborah Winslow and Michael D. Woost (Bloomington: Indiana University Press, 2004).

[2] Ronald Herring, "Explaining Sri Lanka's Exceptionalism: Popular Responses to Welfarism and the Open Economy" in *Free Markets and Food Riots: The Politics of Global Adjustment,* eds., J. Walton and D. Seddon, (Oxford: Blackwells, 1994), 280.

[3] A Sivanandan, "Sri Lanka: Racism and the Politics of Underdevelopment," in *Race & Class* 26, no.1 (1984), 1-37.

[4] Mick Moore, "Economic Liberalisation versus Political Pluralism in Sri Lanka?" in *Modern Asian Studies* 24, no.2 (1990), 341-383 & 377.

[5] Kingsley M. de Silva, *Managing ethnic tensions in multi-ethnic societies: Sri Lanka 1880-1985* (Lanham, Maryland: University Press of America, 1986), 361-2.

plain political conflict and violence.[6] This burgeoning literature has added weight to the suggestion that, though often couched in the discourse of ethnic identity and long-standing rivalries, ethno-political conflict is also shaped by politico-economic structures, relationships, rivalries and incentives. That is, political conflict, even in its most violent manifestations, is inherently, though admittedly not solely, an economic phenomenon. It is argued that war should not be seen as an irrational 'collapse' or 'interruption' to peacetime processes, but should instead be seen as subject to and a product of regular economic forces and processes. This means that the process of economic change cannot be disassociated from the process of political conflict. In short, this literature observes that economic dimensions are useful in understanding why and when ethno-political conflicts occur; that economic factors can shape the dynamics (e.g. intensity, scale, duration, termination) of conflict; and that economic levers can be used in attempts to resolve conflicts. Yet, despite the heuristic potential, such a focus holds for the study of the Sri Lankan conflict, relatively little has been produced in recent years on the political economy of the Sri Lankan conflict. Three reasons for this come to mind.

First, much of the recent literature on the economics of conflict pays little attention to the Sri Lankan case.[7] For a start, many recent studies employ quantitative economic methodologies to analyse multi-national and multi-year empirical data harvested from various data sets on civil wars and related phenomena. The primary focus is thus less on explaining the complex factors at work in particular cases and more on quantifying the relative significance of a large list of variables apparently affecting the likelihood conflict. These 'risk factors,' often quantified to very precise levels, apparently

---

[6] See, e.g., the World Bank's programme on 'The Economics of Civil War, Crime and Violence,' a project on 'Economic Agendas in Civil Wars' hosted by the International Peace Academy, and 'The Political Economy of Civil Wars' project hosted by the International Peace Research Institute, Oslo (PRIO).

[7] See, e.g., Mats Berdal and David Malone, eds., *Greed and Grievance: Economic Agendas in Civil Wars* (Boulder: Lynne Reinner, 2000); Paul Collier, Lani Elliot, Havard Hegre, Anke Hoeffler, Marta Reynal-Querol and Nicholas Sambanis, *Breaking the Conflict Trap: Civil War and Development Policy* (Washington, D.C.: World Bank & Oxford University Press, 2003); Karen Ballentine and Jake Sherman, eds., *The Political Economy of Armed Conflict: Beyond Greed and Grievance* (Boulder, Lynne Rienner, 2003); and a special issue of the *Journal of International Development* 15, no.4 (May 2003).

predict the probability of conflict. However, in the real and changing world, these predictions have little value for individual cases. Much of this new research also has a narrow focus on individual motivations for conflict ('greed') and on the way that natural resources feature in conflict. Since neither issue can be readily identified in the Sri Lankan case (which is often characterised as being motivated by 'grievance'), very little has been written in this regard on Sri Lanka.[8]

Secondly, while studies of the Sri Lankan economy are in abundance, it would seem that, on the whole, Sri Lankan economists 'do not deal with the wider issue of why societies drift into violence.'[9] Instead, they have tended to focus on four particularly intriguing aspects of Sri Lanka's recent economic experience: the regular overhauls in macroeconomic policy directions;[10] the relatively high levels of human development despite low income;[11] a process of market liberalisation without significant reduction in the size of the State,[12] political democratisation,[13] or large scale 'IMF

---

[8] The primary exceptions are instances where the Sri Lankan Diaspora is referred to as a source of funding for rebel movements. See, e.g., Collier *et al.*, *op.cit.*, 2003, 75.

[9] David Dunham and Sisira Jayasuriya, "Equity, Growth and Insurrection: Liberalisation and the Welfare Debate in Contemporary Sri Lanka," in *Oxford Development Studies* 28, no.1 (2000), 97-110 & 98.

[10] Since independence Sri Lankan policy makers have experimented with several economic policy directions. On the one hand, the relatively open, market-oriented stances in the early 1950s and since 1977 and, on the other hand, closed socialistic policies in the early 1970s. See Donald Snodgrass, *The Economic Development of Sri Lanka: A Tale of Missed Opportunities* (Cambridge, MA: Harvard Institute for International Development, 1998); Saman Kelegama, "Development in Independent Sri Lanka: What Went Wrong?" in *Economic and Political Weekly* (22 April 2000), 1477-1490.

[11] Sri Lanka has been relatively successful in education, health care and improving mortality given its relatively low Gross Domestic Product (GDP) per capita (US$3570 in 2002, adjusted for purchasing power). As a result, Sri Lanka's rank on the broader 'Human Development Index' (HDI) (96th out of 177 countries) is 16 places higher than its rank on GDP per capita (UNDP, *Human Development Report 2004* (New York: Oxford University Press, 2004), Table 1, 140.

[12] Sri Lanka has undergone four 'waves' of economic liberalisation: a first starting in 1977 after the election of the United National Party (UNP) government, a second following the re-election of the UNP in 1989, a third following the election of the People's Alliance (PA) in 1994, and a fourth began when the UNP-led coalition was voted in at the Parliamentary elections of December 2001. See David Dunham and Saman Kelegama, *Economic Liberalisation and Structural Reforms: The Experience of Sri Lanka: 1977-93* (The Hague: Institute of Social Studies, 1994); David Dunham and Saman Kelegama, *Economic Reform and Governance: The second wave of liberalisation in Sri Lanka 1989-93* (The Hague: Institute of Social Studies, 1995);

riots;'[14] and the economic impacts of war. As discussed below, much of the focus on this last aspect has been about quantifying the economic costs of war. Studies exploring the material bases of ethno-political conflict in Sri Lanka are few and far between.

Thirdly, within the substantial literature that seeks to describe or explain the Sri Lankan conflict, there seems to be a blind spot when it comes to politico-economic aspects of conflict. This is partly due to the fact that, akin to the misunderstandings of other similar conflicts around the world,[15] many contributions to this body of work are unhelpfully unidimensional. Very often, especially in 'populist' writing, there is an overemphasis on primordial communal hatred as the driving force of conflict. In other cases, there is a narrow focus on the manipulative role of political elites. In both instances, the material conditions that may shape conflict are ignored or considered of secondary importance. Even those studies that do provide a broader analytical framework tend to focus on political and institutional decay, and the cultural and political practices that fuel ethno-political mobilisation,[16] making only passing reference to material factors.

This is *not* to say that economic factors are not judged to be important. On the contrary, there is, as one observer has noted, a consensus 'that economic development policies exacerbated long-

---

alisation in Sri Lanka 1989-93 (The Hague: Institute of Social Studies, 1995); Mick Moore, "The Identity of Capitalists and the Legitimacy of Capitalism: Sri Lanka since Independence," *Development and Change* 28, (1997), 331-366. Despite two decades of economic liberalisation and reform Sri Lanka still has one of the highest rates of public sector employees per capita in the world (World Bank, *op.cit.*,2000: Table 2.2).

[13] David Dunham and Saman Kelegama, "Does Leadership Matter in the Economic Reform Process? Liberalisation and Governance in Sri Lanka, 1989-93," in *World Development* 25, no. 2 (1997), 179-190; Kristian Stokke "Authoritarianism in the age of market liberalism in Sri Lanka," in *Antipode* 29, no.4 (1997), 437-455.

[14] Herring, *op.cit.*, 1994.

[15] Andy Storey "Misunderstanding Ethnicity: Ancient Hatreds, False Consciousness and Rational Choice," in *Irish Journal of Anthropology* 2 (1997), 63-68.

[16] Moore, *op.cit.*, 1990; Sumantra Bose, "States crises and nationalities conflict in Sri Lanka and Yugoslavia," *Comparative Political Studies* 28, no.1 (1995), 87-116; Neil DeVotta, "Control Democracy, Institutional Decay, and the Quest for Eelam: Explaining Ethnic Conflict in Sri Lanka," in *Pacific Affairs* 73, no. 1 (2000), 55-76; Kristian Stokke and A.K. Ryntveit, "The Struggle for Tamil Eelam in Sri Lanka," in *Growth and Change* 31 (Spring 2000), 285-304 & 301.

standing ethnic tensions' in Sri Lanka.[17] What is missing, however, is a cogent literature that articulates the basis for such a consensus. A handful of contributions do seek to explore such factors as competition between Sinhalese and Tamils over access to economic resources such as employment and education,[18] the relationship between class politics and ethnic politics,[19] and the role of material factors in the rise of Tamil nationalism.[20] However, very few studies develop the categories and methodologies to examine the linkages between class, economic development, and ethno-political conflict.[21]

This article seeks to redress these lacunae by exploring what a political economy of Sri Lanka's 'ethnic' conflict might look like. Three specific questions are posed – why did hostilities occur when they did, why has the conflict lasted so long and why has there been a move towards peace lately – and seeks their answers within the process of economic change and development in Sri Lanka. It is suggested that, perhaps contrary to expectations, hostilities in Sri Lanka coincided with a period of relatively high growth, while recent moves towards peace have been preceded by a period of relative stagnation.

---

[17] Greg Alling, "Economic Liberalisation and Separatist Nationalism: The Cases of Sri Lanka and Tibet," in *Journal of International Affairs* 51, no. 1 (1997), in 117-145 &127.

[18] S.W.R. de A Samarasinghe, "Ethnic Representation in Central Government Employment and Sinhala-Tamil Relations in Sri Lanka: 1948-81" in *From Independence to Statehood: Managing Ethnic Conflict in Five African and Asian States*, eds., R. B. Goldmann and A. J. Wilson (London: Frances Pinter, 1984); Kingsley M de Silva, "University Admissions and Ethnic tension in Sri Lanka, 1977-82," in Goldmann and Wilson, ibid., 1984; Lakshmanan Sabaratnam, "Internal Colonies and Their Responses," in *South Asia Bulletin* 6, no. 2 (1986), 3-8.

[19] Kumari Jayawardena, *Ethnic and class conflicts in Sri Lanka: Some aspects of Sinhala Buddhist consciousness over the past 100 years* (Dehiwala: Centre for Social Analysis, 1985); G Anandalingam and Mary Abraham, "Left-wing politics and ethnic conflict in Sri Lanka," in *South Asia Bulletin* 6, no. 2 (1986), 38-45.

[20] V. Nithiyanandan, "An analysis of economic factors behind the origin and development of Tamil nationalism in Sri Lanka," in Abeysekera and Gunasinghe, *op.cit.*, 1984; Amita Shastri, "The Material Basis for Separation: The Tamil Eelam Movement in Sri Lanka," in *The Sri Lankan Tamils: Ethnicity and Identity*, eds., C. Manogaran and Brian Pfaffenberger (Boulder: Westview, 1994); Siri Gamage, "Radicalisation of the Tamil Middle Class and Ethnic Violence in Sri Lanka," *Journal of Contemporary Asia* 24, no. 2 (1994), 161-178.

[21] Radhika Coomaraswamy, "Linkages between methodology, research and theory in race and ethnic studies: a case study of Sri Lanka," in *"Race," Ethnicity and National: International Perspectives on Social Conflict*, ed., P. Ratcliffe (London: UCL Press, 1994).

Analytically, it is suggested that the study of conflict in Sri Lanka needs to pay attention to changes and contradictions in Sri Lanka's economic development, particularly in the development of new politico-economic spaces and scales.[22]

At the heart of this approach is the belief that, though the existence of ethnic or other difference may be a fundamental feature of most inter-group conflicts, it is by no means a sufficient condition. Instead, it is suggested that there are important forces informed by instrumentalist concerns with political and economic power that will impact on the nature and extent of ethno-political mobilisation and conflict. Indeed, politico-economic institutions are both the *subject* of controversy in conflicts and also the *means* by which resolution can be sought. By interrogating the relationship between economy and society, especially the processes, policies, interests, and impacts through which the material and the political interact, this article aims to move towards a political economy of the ethno-political conflict in Sri Lanka.

The article cannot and does not claim to explain conclusively why ethnic tensions exist in the first place, nor the ways in which tensions are fuelled or ameliorated by political processes and institutions. It is also not an attempt to quantify or model economic aspects of conflict. Instead, like Gunasinghe's work, this is an attempt to consider the economic while moving beyond narrow economistic assumptions about rational private motivations and methodologies that seek out empirical regularities. The rationale is that 'economic forces continue to dominate contemporary life, and thus, however unfashionable, economic analysis cannot be sidelined.'[23] The challenge is to turn the tables; to deploy economic methodologies to emphasise factors that non-economists have been concerned with for generations.[24] In doing so, it will also be useful to recover the politi-

---

[22] Bob Jessop, "The Crisis of the National Spatio-Temporal Fix and the Tendential Ecological Dominance of Globalising Capitalism," in *International Journal of Urban and Regional Research* 24, no. 2 (2000), 323-360.

[23] Andrew Sayer, "The Dialectic of Culture and Economy," in *Geographies of Economies*, eds., R. Lee & J. Wills, (London: Arnold, 1997), 16.

[24] Ben Fine, "Economics Imperialism and Intellectual Progress: The Present as History of Economic Thought?" in *History of Economics Review* 32 (Summer 2000), 10-35.

cal economy that Gunasinghe and others used to explore inequality, development and power in Sri Lanka and elsewhere.

Such a project must acknowledge that economic processes are open-ended and not pre-determined, not least as a result of humans making their own past, present and future rather than these being ground out by some deterministic model. Much of the content of mainstream economic theory, not least its particular form of methodological individualism and its emphasis on equilibrium as an organising concept, are rendered unhelpfully reductionist. [25] Instead, 'to the extent that regularities in the social realm exist to be identified or theorised about, there will be a plurality of partial realities and processes of underlying events.'[26] Rather than foolishly seek predictable or universal regularities, this article seeks to explore the generative mechanisms, structures, and powers that have shaped the ethno-political conflict in Sri Lanka. Such a view not only precludes the design and testing of a strong hypothesis but, given the modest scope of what can be achieved here, also means the aim is to make observations and not conclusions or predictions about how economic factors have shaped the conflict in Sri Lanka.

WHY DID HOSTILITIES OCCUR WHEN THEY DID?

Sri Lanka's population is highly heterogeneous: differentiated across ethnic, religious, linguistic, caste and regional lines. Yet, despite this diversity, ethnicity has been the most important basis for official ascription, collective self-identification and political conflict. For decades, Tamil political leaders had been voicing concerns about their exclusion from political power, discriminatory State policies, incidents of anti-Tamil violence, broken promises by Sinhalese leaders, and State-sponsored Sinhalese settlement in Tamil areas. For its part, the State had made clear its intolerance of Tamil separatism and militancy. In the context of rising tensions between the Sinhalese and

---

[25] Tony Lawson, "Two Responses to the Failings of Modern Economics: the Instrumentalist and the Realist," in *Review of Population and Social Policy* 10 (2001), 155-181.
[26] Paul Downward, John H. Finch, and John Ramsay, "Critical realism, empirical methods and inference: a critical discussion," in *Cambridge Journal of Economics* 26 (2001), 481-500.

Northeastern Tamils,[27] the anti-Tamil pogrom of 1983 and the subsequent escalation in the civil war may not have been particularly surprising. Yet, in other ways, the scale of the riots and the intensity of the Tamil militant response do require explanation.

From an economic perspective, Sri Lanka was undergoing considerable upheaval as a result of economic liberalisation policies. Drawing out the links between economic liberalisation and the sharpening of ethnic tensions was one of the primary aims of the two essays by Gunasinghe, 'The Open Economy & Its Impact on Ethnic Relations in Sri Lanka' (hereafter OE) and 'Ethnic Conflict in Sri Lanka: Perceptions and Solutions' (hereafter EC).[28]

Gunasinghe's compelling account of the increase in ethnic hostilities in Sri Lanka from the late 1970s explores the impacts of Sri Lanka's transition from a State-regulated economic system between 1955-1977 to an 'open' economy initiated by the newly elected United National Party (UNP) government from 1977. The new government set about overhauling the political system, largely through the enactment of a second autochthonous Constitution, and economic policy, through a program of economic liberalisation. **While economic restructuring was sporadic and often incomplete, it did result in (1) opening up of an economy that had been virtually closed to the outside world during the rule of the previous regime (1970-77) and (2) cuts in the social welfare programmes.** These policies, Gunasinghe argues, had unexpected and differential impacts which are key to explaining why inter-ethnic hostilities increased in the years from 1977 to 1983.

The Sinhalese business middle class, a group that had been dependent upon quotas and licenses for protected domestic production under the previous regime, found it hard to compete against cheaper and better quality imports (OE). Apart from these adverse

---

[27] An important distinction is drawn between those Tamil-speaking people of Sri Lanka who reside in or originate from the island's Northeast (often called 'Sri Lankan Tamils' in official literature) and those who live in upcountry areas in the South whose ancestors migrated from India primarily to work on tea plantations (sometimes called 'Indian Tamil').

[28] Originally published in the Indian magazine *Frontline* (23 March-5 April 1985), this essay has been reproduced in *South Asia Bulletin* 6, no.2 (1986), 34-37; in Abeysekera and Gunasinghe (eds.), *op.cit.*, 1987; and in *Sociology of Developing Societies: South Asia*, eds., Hamza Alawi and John Harriss (London: Macmillan, 1989).

effects, this group also found themselves, in the absence of the political patronage they had hitherto enjoyed, doing relatively worse than Tamil and Muslim entrepreneurs, many of whom were occupied in the trading sector and were reaping the benefits of increased international trade. Gunasinghe contends that the Sinhalese entrepreneurial middle-class, along with ethnic allies amongst professionals, monks and the rural intelligentsia, were key in propagating the 'mytho-ideological' doctrine that underpinned Sinhala-Buddhist chauvinism (EC).

The cutting of benefits had an adverse impact on the average citizen, said to have become 'the most subsidised creature in the world' during the 1970s.[29] While the entire economy was growing (see Table 1), the economic lives of the lower classes were becoming more uncertain. For everyone concerned, the general concessions of old were abolished and replaced by a new patron-client system in which only a few gained.[30] This process of economic upheaval did little to address the unmet expectations and frustrations, especially amongst youth, that had already resulted in a spectacular but unsuccessful youth insurrection against the State led by the Janatha Vimukthi Peruma (JVP) in the early 1970s.[31] According to Gunasinghe, the period of economic liberalisation not only made the Sinhalese urban poor more volatile, but also left them open to mobilisation by Sinhala-Buddhist chauvinists (OE). The State, which had hitherto been the target of protest, was now superseded by a new target: the seemingly prosperous Sri Lankan Tamil minority.

A third element of the argument deals with the adverse impact of this economic policy on the Jaffna middle peasantry. Increased yields and protective trade policies had led to rapid increases in Northeast rural incomes,[32] especially from the sale of non-paddy

---

[29] Mervyn de Silva, "Sri Lanka: The End of Welfare Politics," in *South Asia Review* 6, no. 2 (1973).

[30] Herring, *op.cit.*, 1994, 268-271.

[31] W.H. Wriggins and C.H.S. Jayewardene, "Youth Protest in Sri Lanka (Ceylon)," in *Population, Politics and the Future of Southern Asia*, eds., W. H. Wriggins and J. F. Goyot (New York: Columbia University Press, 1973); Gananath Obeyesekere, "Some Comments on the Social Backgrounds of the April 1971 Insurgency in Sri Lanka (Ceylon)," in *Journal of Asian Studies* 33, no. 3 (1974), 367-384.

[32] For example, in 1973, cultivators of food crops in the Northeast had an average income of Rs. 173 per month, far higher than other districts (G. I. O. M. Kurukulas-

crops such as chillies and onions.[33] In turn, this boom in rural incomes may have artificially buoyed the Northeastern economy during the early 1970s; a time when trend-relative incomes were falling in other sectors and regions. With the change in policy of the UNP government from 1977, cheaper imports began to undercut the North's share of the market in these products. This hurt Northeastern farmers and had an adverse flow-on effect on incomes in the region's economy at a time of growing political and social volatility. The situation was made worse by the imposition of curfews and other military restrictions that limited economic activity in the Northeast (EC). Worsening economic conditions, in addition to perceptions of State discrimination against Tamils in public sector employment and tertiary education, added to the growing frustrations of non-propertied lower-middle-class Tamil youth – the very group that were readily recruited into Tamil militant groups (EC). In the political sphere, the Tamil leaders who had articulated the economic potential of the Northeast during the period of relative economic boom were now blaming economic stagnation on State discrimination and fuelling Tamil nationalism.[34]

In sum, by exploring the economic context, Gunasinghe unmasks economic aspects of ostensibly 'ethnic' hostilities and paves the way for accounts of conflict that do not rely solely on the politics of identity. In particular, the analysis highlights important spatiotemporal process such as the internationalisation of national economic space. He also questions the temporal assumption 'that ethnic conflicts are more likely to erupt into open violence during phases of economic depression.' Instead, he seeks out the 'linkages between economic structure and ethnic contradictions' (OE). That Gunasinghe's analytical approach was not followed up in any systematic way does not imply that the approach was not useful, or that economic factors have become any less important. Instead, factors such as Gunasinghe's untimely death, the dispersal of the Leftist circle of

---

uriya, *An Analytical Description of Poverty in Sri Lanka*, (Colombo: Marga Institute, 1982), 89). Agricultural labourers in the Northeast also enjoyed some of the highest incomes in the country.
[33] C. Manogaran, *Ethnic Conflict and Reconciliation in Sri Lanka* (Honolulu: University of Hawaii Press, 1987), 138-9.
[34] Shastri, *op.cit.*, 1994

which he was a prominent part, a shift away from Marxist perspectives, and the emergence in Sri Lanka of a new batch of young economists trained in neoclassical economics have all meant that the priorities identified in Gunasinghe's work have not been pursued fully. Nor, importantly, have the sorts of questions he posed been asked of more recent developments in the history of Sri Lanka's conflict. We turn to two such questions now.

WHY DID THE WAR LAST SO LONG?

Before turning to the specific question how economic factors may have facilitated the length of the Sri Lankan conflict, it is worth noting a key set of differences in the assessment of Sri Lanka's economic performance in recent decades. In general, such assessments stress either *sub-optimality*, especially resulting from factors such as policy inconsistencies, corruption and the impact of war, or *relative robustness*, citing high growth rates and human development achievements despite many challenges. Much depends on what time frame is adopted and what comparators are used.

From a long-term perspective, it is clear that Sri Lanka's progress has not lived up to expectations. Around the time of the country's independence, Sri Lanka was considered to be the 'best bet in Asia' to achieve rapid economic development.[35] Yet, despite its early advantage and promise, Sri Lanka has fallen well behind the 'tiger' economies of East and Southeast Asia, making it commonplace to talk of the 'missed opportunities' that have plagued Sri Lanka's development.[36] Narrowing the focus to recent decades, it is possible to observe Sri Lanka's descent into a vicious spiral of war and underdevelopment that has resulted in the country falling further behind the rest of Asia, the world's fastest growing region. Sri Lanka's average GDP growth per capita between 1975 and 2002 was 3.4 per cent per annum, while the East Asia and Pacific region grew at 5.9 per cent per annum.[37]

On the other hand, Sri Lanka has managed to maintain relative advantage over its South Asian neighbours. It has also made and

---

[35] Kelegama, *op.cit.*, 2000, 1477.
[36] World Bank, *Sri Lanka: Recapturing Missed Opportunities* (Washington, D.C.: World Bank, 2000); Snodgrass, *op.cit.*, 1988.

sustained significant achievements in meeting the basic needs of a large proportion of the population and equitable distribution.[38] When compared to other developing countries plagued by large-scale internal wars, Sri Lanka has managed to perform relatively well in terms of growth and development.[39] Indeed, the Sri Lankan economy grew at a faster rate in the midst of civil war than before the outbreak of war[40] and socio-economic upheaval caused by war has not been as great as might have been expected.[41]

While war may find its roots in the sphere of politics, it finds its sustenance in the economy. An examination of economic conditions over the last two decades reveals some clues as to why the Sri Lankan conflict lasted as long as it did (has). Three particular observations are worth noting: the two main protagonists (and the economy as a whole) were able to mobilise the required financial resources to wage war; the economic impacts of war were not, in general, adverse enough to consolidate opposition to war; and key stakeholders derived economic benefits from war. With the usual caveat that such observations can only ever paint part of the picture, the door is left open to the possibility that, in Sri Lanka, war has made economic sense: it was financially feasible, not overtly costly and actually beneficial to some.

ECONOMIC GROWTH

Two decades of war have come at considerable cost. At the macro-scale, there has been significant loss, disruption and curtailment of production. Sri Lanka's military expenditure, though difficult to estimate accurately,[42] has consistently stood at around 5 per

---

[37] UNDP, *op.cit.*, 2004, Table 13, 184-187.

[38] Paul Isenman, "Basic Needs: The Case of Sri Lanka," in *World Development,* no. 8 (1980), 237-258; S.R. Osmani, "Is there a Conflict Between Growth and Welfarism? The Significance of the Sri Lanka Debate," in *Development and Change* 25 (1994), 387-421.

[39] Meghan O'Sullivan, "Household Entitlements During Wartime: The Experience of Sri Lanka," *Oxford Development Studies* 25, no. 1 (1997), 95-121.

[40] Sri Lanka had an average annual GDP growth rate of 4.1% between 1951-1982, and a rate of 4.3% between 1983-2002 (Central Bank of Sri Lanka 2003).

[41] Dunham and Jayasuriya, *op.cit.*, 2000.

[42] M. Sarvananthan, "The International Monetary Fund in Sri Lanka: a Critical Dialogue," in *Contemporary South Asia* 11, no.1 (2002), 77-88.

cent of GDP during the late 1990s (see Figure 1), the highest level in South Asia and one of the highest in the world.[43] There has also been higher than normal spending on relief and rehabilitation as a result of the war. Although these expenditures have been funded in part through additional tax burdens,[44] there has been a gradual fall in other areas of public expenditure, especially in economic services (Figure 1). At the micro-scale, local economies, especially in the Northeast, have been disrupted,[45] individuals have found it difficult to pursue their livelihoods, and there have been limited opportunities for human development, particularly because of disruption to education. There have also been significant costs associated with the destruction of economic infrastructure and the disruption of economic life due to curfews and road closures.

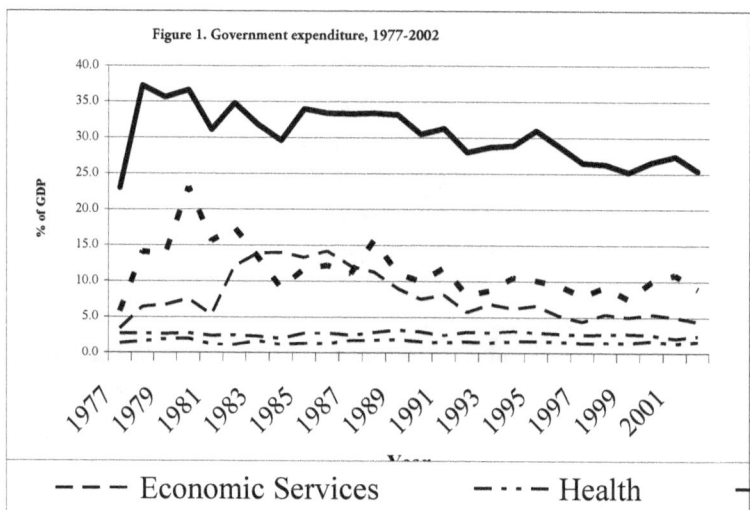

Figure 1. Government expenditure, 1977-2002

Figure 1

---

[43] National Peace Council Sri Lanka, *The Cost of War* (Colombo: National Peace Delegates Convention, 4 January 1998), 9)

[44] For example, the Government sought to fund rising expenditure during the 1990s through the imposition of a direct Defence Levy (called the National Security Levy from 1995).

[45] Paul Seabright, "The Effects of Conflict on the Economy of Northern Sri Lanka," in *Economic and Political Weekly* 21, no. 2 (1986), 78-83.

There have been several attempts to calculate the costs of conflict in Sri Lanka. According to one estimate,[46] the quantifiable cost of the war was around US$16 billion for the period 1983-1994 (1995 dollars), a figure that accounts for about 131 per cent of total 1995 GDP.[47] Another study estimates that annual GDP growth between 1983-1996 could have been as high as 7 per cent per annum, much higher than the actual rate of 4.3 per cent.[48] This extra growth would have added 41 per cent to average household income at the end of the period. The insecurity and political uncertainty caused by the war has, despite several positive measures to attract export-oriented FDI since 1977 and again since 1989, led to sub-optimal levels of foreign investment. It has been argued that Sri Lanka could have attracted a further US$1 billion in FDI between 1984-96, thus doubling actual flows,[49] and that the cumulative lost earnings from passed up investment totalled around US$9 billion (1996 dollars).[50] Sri Lanka's political problems were also badly timed in terms of developments in the global economy, with the island missing out on potentially lucrative investment in the electronics industry and on becoming a destination for Japan's Yen surpluses in the late 1980s.[51]

However, it is particularly notable that, despite the scale of these costs, the post-1983 period has seen consistent economic

[46] Saman Kelegama, "Economic Costs of Conflict in Sri Lanka," in *Creating Peace in Sri Lanka: Civil War and Reconciliation*, ed., Robert Rotberg (Washington, D.C.: Brookings Institution, 1999), 79.

[47] An older estimate put the opportunity cost of the war between 1983-1988 at US$1.5 billion and estimated that were the war to continue to 1995 this figure would rise to between $US7-15 billion (both figures in 1988 dollars). L. M. Grobar and S. Gnanaselvam, "The Economic Effects of the Sri Lankan Civil War," in *Economic Development and Cultural Change* 41, no. 2 (1993), 395-405.

[48] National Peace Council Sri Lanka, *op.cit.*, 1998, 31.

[49] *Ibid.*, 21.

[50] Nisha Arunatilake, Sisira Jayasuriya and Saman Kelegama, "The Economic Cost of the War in Sri Lanka," in *World Development* 29, no. 9 (2001), 1483-1500.

[51] One example is the case of Motorola and the Harris Corporation, two multinational electronics firms that withdrew from Sri Lanka in 1980s while in the process of establishing manufacturing operations (P. Athukorala, "Foreign Direct Investment and manufacturing for Export in a New Exporting country: The case of Sri Lanka," in *The World Economy* 18, no.4 (1995), 543-564 & p.553). More broadly, it has been argued that Sri Lanka missed out on inflows of Japanese investment, something the Southeast Asian countries benefited from, from the late 1980s (Kelegama, *op.cit.*, 1999, 75).

growth and improvements in human development. Average GDP growth of over 5 per cent per annum from 1983-2001 (Table 1) is a remarkable feat for any country, let alone one that was experiencing a civil war. Similarly, Sri Lanka's performance on welfare indicators such as literacy, nutrition and life expectancy are amongst the best in the developing world and higher than any of its South Asian neighbours. Similarly, rates of capital formation, an important indicator of the health of an economy, have remained healthy at between 20 per cent and 30 per cent of GDP throughout this period (Table 1), on par or better than all the countries of the region except Bangladesh.[52] The war also does not seem to have hindered the structural transformation of the economy and the rapid growth in manufacturing. There has been a steady increase in the contribution of the industrial and service sectors of the economy, as agriculture's relative economic contribution has waned.[53]

ECONOMIC GEOGRAPHY

An account of how such economic growth was possible needs to take into account two important spatial factors: the internationalisation of Sri Lanka's economy since 1977, and the isolation of the Northeast during years of civil war. First, while it has been suggested that the 'very boldness' of Sri Lanka's liberalisation strategy was dependent on international support,[54] few would have predicted in 1977 the degree to which this has happened. Foreign aid levels were substantial at key periods (Table 1), especially in the late 1980s and early 1990s, and were used to fund key infrastructure projects and stimulate economic growth.[55]

---

[52] Asian Development Bank, *op.cit.*, 2002, Table 15, 61.
[53] During the 1990s the leading contributors to GDP growth were the service (54.5%) and manufacturing (29.9%) sectors (World Bank, *op.cit.*, 2000, A3).
[54] Herring, *op.cit.*, 1994, 269.
[55] B. Levy, *Foreign Aid in the Making of Economic Policy in Sri Lanka 1977-83*, (Williamstown, MA: Centre for Development Economics, Williams College, 1987).

Table 1: Sri Lanka: selected economic indicators, 1977-2002

	1977	1978	1979	1980	1981	1982	1983	1984	1985
1. GDP growth (annual %)	5.1	5.7	6.4	5.8	5.7	4.1	4.8	5.1	5.0
2. Household final consumption per capita growth (annual %)	10.9	-3.0	-3.0	2.0	10.2	4.3	15.0	0.0	-1.5
3. Inflation, consumer prices (annual %)	1.2	12.1	10.7	26.1	18.0	10.8	14.0	16.6	1.5
4. Gross capital formation (% of GDP)	14.4	20.0	25.8	33.8	27.8	30.8	28.9	25.8	22.2
5. Exports of goods and services (% of GDP)	33.8	34.8	33.7	32.2	30.5	27.4	26.3	28.8	26.0
6. FDI net inflows (current US$ mill)	-1	2	46	43	49	64	38	33	26
(% of GDP)	0.0	0.1	1.4	1.1	1.1	1.3	0.7	0.5	0.4
7. ODA & official aid (current US$ mill)	187	324	323	390	377	416	471	457	468
(% of GDP)	4.5	11.9	9.6	9.7	8.5	8.7	9.1	7.6	7.8
8. Workers' remittances receipts (current US$mill)	18	39	60	152	230	289	294	301	292
(% of GDP)	0.4	1.4	1.8	3.8	5.2	6.1	5.7	5.0	4.9
9. Government expenditure (% of GDP)	23.0	37.2	35.6	36.6	31.1	34.8	31.8	29.6	34
10. Budget deficit (% of GDP)	5.8	14.1	13.8	23.1	15.6	17.4	13.4	9.0	11.7
11. Economic services expenditure (% of GDP)	3.4	6.4	6.7	7.5	5.3	12.1	13.9	14.0	13.3
12. Defence expenditure as % of GDP	-	-	-	-	-	-	-	-	2.9

1987	1988	1989	1990	1991	1992	1993	1994
1.7	2.5	2.3	6.4	4.6	4.4	6.9	5.6
0.4	1.0	-0.6	1.6	5.7	3.5	6.1	5.1
7.7	14.0	11.6	21.5	12.2	11.4	11.7	8.4
23.3	22.8	21.7	22.2	22.9	24.3	25.6	27.0
25.2	26.1	27.3	30.2	28.7	31.8	33.8	33.8
60	46	20	43	48	123	195	166
0.9	*0.7*	*0.3*	*0.5*	*0.5*	*1.3*	*1.9*	*1.4*
477	635	620	730	890	639	659	595
7.1	*9.1*	*8.9*	*9.1*	*9.9*	*6.6*	*6.4*	*5.1*
350	358	358	401	442	548	632	715
5.2	*5.1*	*5.1*	*5.0*	*4.9*	*5.6*	*6.1*	*6.1*
33.3	33.4	33.2	30.5	31.3	28.0	28.7	28.9
11.1	15.7	11.2	9.9	11.9	8.0	8.7	10.5
12.1	11.3	9.0	7.5	8.1	5.7	6.8	6.2
3.1	4.6	4.3	4.8	4.9	3.8	4.1	4.7

1995	1996	1997	1998	1999	2000	2001	2002
5.5	3.8	6.4	4.7	4.3	6.0	-1.4	3.0
1.9	4.2	5.6	6.2	5.2	-	-	-
7.7	15.9	9.6	9.4	4.7	6.2	14.2	9.6
25.7	24.2	24.4	25.1	27.1	28.1	22.0	23.0
35.6	35.0	36.5	36.2	35.3	39.7	37.0	-
56	120	430	193	177	173	172	233e
0.4	0.9	2.9	1.3	1.1	1.0	1.1	-
553	485	329	490	251	276	330	-
4.3	3.5	2.2	3.2	1.6	1.7	2.1	-
790	832	922	999	1056	1160	1155	1287
6.2	6.0	6.2	6.5	6.6	7.0	7.3	-
31.0	28.8	26.5	26.3	25.2	26.6	27.4	25.4
10.1	9.4	7.9	9.2	7.5	9.9	10.9	8.9
6.6	5.2	4.4	5.4	5.0	5.4	5.0	4.4
6.4	5.9	5.1	5.0	4.3	4.0p	--	-

Source: For rows 1-8 & 12, data for 1983-1999 are from *World Development Indicators (WDI)* CD-ROM (Washington D.C.: World Bank, 2001). Data for 2000-2 for rows 1,4 & 5 are from *WDI 2003* (online); for row 3 are from *Key Indicators 2002: Population and Human Resource Trends and Challenges* (Manila: Asian Development Bank, 2002), Table 18, p.65; for rows 6 & 7 from *Human Development Report* (New York: United Nations Development Programme, 2003); and for row 8 from Central Bank of Sri Lanka *Annual Report 2002*, Statistical Appendix, Table 99. All figures in rows 9-11 are from Central Bank of Sri Lanka *Annual Report 2002*, Special Statistical Appendix: tables 20 & 21. All data for 2002 are provisional.

While total levels of foreign direct investment (FDI) into Sri Lanka have not been particularly high, averaging only around 1 per cent of GDP from 1983-1999 (Table 1), the contribution of exports has grown significantly. At times where the tourism sector has been adversely affected by the war, exports have continued almost unabated. The most spectacular growth since 1977 has been in manufacturing exports, and the strongest sub-sector has been garments.[56] In 1977, there were 5 garment factories earning US$10 million in exports. By 2000, Sri Lanka had 890 factories, earning US$2.7 billion and making up some 54 per cent of total exports.[57]

The massive expansion of labour migration, primarily to the Middle East, during the 1980s has also served as an important economic 'safety valve.' Facilitated by State policy that encourages short-term migration, there are now nearly one million Sri Lankans living overseas, many of whom work in the domestic and construction sectors. This group sends home well over US$1 billion annually in official remittances, accounting for more than 6 per cent of Sri Lanka's GDP.[58] Apart from being a major contribution to Sri Lanka's foreign exchange reserves, these remittances bolster the household incomes of migrants' families. Labour migration, together with military recruitment (see below), has also been vital in reducing domestic unemployment rates, especially in the rural South. Similarly, large flows of private remittances from the Tamil diaspora (estimated to over 500,000 people) to support kith and kin in Sri Lanka have been undeniably important to the domestic economy, both in the Northeast and in areas where Tamils have been internally displaced.

In sum, these international financial inflows allowed the economy to ameliorate some of the potentially adverse economic impacts of war. More directly, these foreign flows have allowed the main protagonists to sustain a war beyond their domestic capacity. The result has been sustained and, at times, escalating war. At the outset of hostilities, when the costs of resisting a guerrilla campaign

---

[56] Saman Kelegama and Roshen Epaarachchi, *Productivity, Competitiveness and Job Quality in Garment Industry in Sri Lanka* (New Delhi: International Labour Organisation, 2000).

[57] *Ibid.*

[58] Dhananjayan Sriskandarajah, "The migration-development nexus: Sri Lanka case study," in *International Migration* 40, no. 5 (2002), 283-307.

were small, the Sri Lankan State drew on existing resources. For their part, the fledgling Tamil militants drew considerable initial support from India.[59] However, both sides' subsequent expansion has been funded in part by taxation of the areas under their control but also, importantly, by foreign financial flows. For the Sri Lankan State, aid, remittances and export earnings were directly important in supplying the foreign exchange needed to purchase of military hardware.[60] Similarly, while the evidence on LTTE (The Liberation Tigers of Tamil Eelam) finance is highly speculative, it is certain that the LTTE is just as much, if not more, reliant on foreign finance, largely from private contributions from the sizeable Tamil diaspora resident in the West and from its own commercial ventures.[61]

Secondly, it is important to note that almost all fighting, and the resulting destruction and disruption, has been restricted to the Northeast of the island. The rest of the island suffered relatively little direct physical and economic damage.[62] Thus, while those who remained in the Northeast often had little choice but to bear the heavy brunt of war, those in the rest of the island were largely exempt from these direct effects. Indeed, it could even be argued that the rest of the island benefited from the economic isolation of the Northeast. For a start, the removal of the Northeast did not have any significant supply-side impacts on the rest of the economy. In terms of agricul-

---

[59] Kingsley M. de Silva and R. J. May, eds., *Internationalisation of Ethnic Conflict* (London: Pinter, 1991), see especially chapters by Shelton Kodiakara and S. D. Muni.
[60] In a more indirect sense, aid, for example, was used to fund projects, such as large-scale irrigation that were perceived by Tamils as supporting the settlement of the Sinhalese in traditionally Tamil areas, that had incendiary implications. See Ronald Herring, "Making Ethnic Conflict: The Civil War in Sri Lanka," in *Carrots, Sticks and Ethnic Conflict. Rethinking Development Assistance*, eds., Milton J. Esman and Ronald Herring (Ann Arbor: University of Michigan Press, 2001).
[61] In a more narrow sense, the wages and pensions paid by the Government to many in the Northeast, even at the height of the war, were an important source of liquidity in an otherwise dysfunctional economy (O'Sullivan, *op.cit.*, 1997, 106). While no figures are available, it could be deduced that this was another source of external income into the Northeast that played an important role in financing the LTTE, directly through taxation and indirectly through circulation.
[62] Indeed, since 1990, the Northeast has also been cut off in accounting terms, meaning that much of the adverse impacts of war and cost of redressing those impacts were not cost in national accounts. On the other hand, the military expenditure assigned to operations in the Northeast did contribute to GDP. Since the 2002 ceasefire, the cost of reconstruction and rehabilitation features again in national accounts.

ture, while the peninsula was a net supplier of many types of produce to the rest of the island, the availability of cheaper overseas imports after liberalisation and the general reduction in the economic importance of agriculture has meant that reduced production in the Northeast has not affected the rest of the island greatly.[63] Moreover, the Northeast was home to few of the activities (garments; manufacturing) that have been the engines of recent growth. Only a few large-scale public infrastructure projects were located in the Northeast and most of these were extractive industries. Of these, the Kankesanthurai cement factory, which supplied 39 per cent of the island's cement needs in 1982, was by far the most important.[64] While the outbreak of hostilities led eventually to the complete closure of the plant, the growth in imports and in the output from Southern plants mitigated any adverse impact that reduced supply may have had on the rest of the island. The fact that some of these imports were cheaper than what was likely to have been produced at Kankesanthurai meant the war had, at least in this instance, led to a more economically efficient outcome.

WELFARISM

Despite the strength of the political support for war against the LTTE amongst the Sinhalese electorate, it might have been expected that if the costs of war were substantial, particularly amongst the poor, enthusiasm for war would have been diminished. However, there is evidence to suggest that, instead of being adversely affected by war, Sri Lanka's rural poor actually improved their economic position during the war years. GDP growth has been accompanied by rising private consumption (see Table 1) and slight falls in income

---

[63] There is some evidence to suggest that restrictions on fishing in the Northeast may have had a potentially negative impact. Given the relative importance of the Northeastern catch (it accounted for nearly 60 per cent of the island's fish before the war broke out (Kelegama, *op.cit.*, 1999, 76)), the estimated falls of 12 per cent per annum in the early 1990s may have pushed up consumer prices for fish in the South (UNDP, *National Human Development Report: Sri Lanka 1998* (Colombo: UNDP, 1998). If this was indeed the case, more research is needed to ascertain the net economic impact of this fall in supply, taking into account a potential increase in the incomes of Southern fishing communities, some of Sri Lanka's poorest groups. Similarly, the fact that the Northeast was a net importer of food at times during the war may have pushed up producer prices in the South.

[64] Seabright, *op.cit.*, 1986, 81.

inequality since the late 1980s. Rural poverty, though fluctuating, was lower at the end of the 1990s than during the 1980s.[65]

The most important reason for this has been a commitment by successive sri lankan governments to initiate or sustain welfare measures primarily aimed at the largely sinhalese rural poor. While it has been argued that the process of economic liberalisation in Sri Lanka has been imbued with populist policies from the very start,[66] the war situation led to a unique set of circumstances. In fiscal terms, Sri Lanka is said to be one of the few countries in the world that has significantly increased military expenditure while simultaneously increasing spending on health and education.[67] As a result, expenditure in these two areas has been stable as a percentage of GDP for the last two decades (see Figure 1). There has also been internal redistribution within budget lines to favour activities that are likely to bolster popular support. For example, expenditure on primary and secondary education has been increased at the cost of spending on the tertiary sector.[68]

The State has also devoted huge resources to poverty alleviation and boosting rural incomes through initiatives such as the *Janasaviya* Programme and the *Samurdhi* Development Programme. The latter covers some two million households (80 per cent of whom receive a direct transfer), accounts for around 1 per cent of total GDP, and has itself generated some 30,000 jobs.[69] Such measures have been critical in ensuring that, even during times of stagnating average private consumption in the late 1980s, there was falling poverty and rising consumption in rural areas.

Successive Sri Lankan governments have also used development schemes to further political objectives. For example, liberalisation 'through a somewhat round-about process of attracting foreign donors that jumped at the prospect of a democracy decentralising its State-led economy, in reality allowed the State to undertake a massive development project [the Mahaweli scheme] aimed at a further

---

[65] World Bank, *op.cit.*, 2000, A15.
[66] Herring, *op.cit.*, 1994.
[67] Third World Institute, *Social Watch 2003* (Montivideo: Third World Institute, 2003).
[68] O'Sullivan, *op.cit.*, 1997, 101-2.
[69] Rozana Salih, *The Samurdhi Poverty Alleviation Scheme* (Geneva: ILO, 2000), 22.

deepening of the Sinhala nationalist view of Sri Lanka.'[70] Further, ideological activities associated with nationalism have also featured more widely in development policy and practice (e.g. 'grass roots' strategies such as Sarvodaya).[71] In sum, a heady mix of nationalist discourse and economic crumbs has undermined the potential for the poor to disrupt the 'war economy.'

FUNCTIONALITY

Another key aspect of the development of a 'war economy' in Sri Lanka is the direct material gains made by key groups. Such a claim goes one step further than the claim made above – that the State sought to dampen any potential resistance to war efforts – and posits that some sections of the population actually had an incentive to support the war effort.

First, the war has generated lucrative sources of employment. The total numbers employed in the military (the three forces plus the police) rose from 58,600 in 1986 to 235,000 in 1996,[72] a four-fold increase over a decade. The incomes and pensions of military personnel[73] are estimated to have supported some 720,000 people in rural Sri Lanka in 1998, and a further 400,000 new jobs (many in private security services) are said to have been created as a result of the war.[74] While this employment generation, like large-scale labour migration, represented an economic 'safety valve' it also had an important political dimension. Given that most military recruits came from the same lower-middle class socio-economic backgrounds as the JVP,[75] it could be argued that this recruitment 'crowded out' recruitment of disgruntled youth into radical organisations.

Secondly, the war has opened up new and, arguably, more lucrative opportunities for rent seeking. These range from bribe taking

---

[70] Alling, *op.cit.*, 1997, 129.
[71] Michael D. Woost, "Nationalizing the Local Past in Sri Lanka: Histories of Nation and Development in a Sinhalese Village," in *American Ethnologist* 20, no. 3 (1993), 502-521.
[72] Kelegama, *op.cit.*, 1999, Table 5-3, 75.
[73] Military incomes are generally several times more than average incomes in recruiting areas and, in case of death, a recruit's family is guaranteed a pension until the recruit would have turned 55 years of age.
[74] "Sri Lanka Blood and money" in *The Economist* 8 (August 1998), 38.
[75] Gamage, *op.cit.*, 1994, 172.

by minor officials at checkpoints to allegations of senior officials receiving sizeable 'kickbacks' in arms deals.[76] The existence of an em-
bargo on the flow of numerous goods to the Northeast also created a
lucrative source of income for smugglers.

Thirdly, there were expanded opportunities for those supplying goods and services that were in greater demand as a result of the
war. For example, domestic suppliers of key military inputs ranging
from uniforms to foodstuffs have benefited from lucrative contracts.
Businesses and landlords in areas where the displaced Tamil population settled also benefited. This includes 'border' towns such as Va-
vuniya, once a sleepy township and now a hub of military and
civilian activity, and Colombo, where the real estate market in some
suburbs sky-rocketed in recent years. The fact that many of the displaced are amongst the richer sections of the Northeast Tamils (with
the means to leave the war zone) and/or are supported by Diaspora
remittances has meant that their combined financial contribution to
the Colombo economy, especially through purchases of consumer
goods, has been substantial.

In analytical terms, Sri Lanka's 'war economy' could be said
to involve a deepening of the *rapprochement* between the Sinhalese
political and economic elites that has taken place in recent decades.[77]
Shared interests between the two groups have shaped the transition
to capitalist economic policies since 1977 but may also have reduced
the risk of contradictions that could have undermined the post-1983
'war economy.' Something akin to the so-called 'military-industrial
complex' has emerged. However, in this tiny outpost on the periph-
ery of the global capitalist system, the complex exists on a much
smaller scale and, rather than a few large corporations benefiting,
there are a more diffuse set of beneficiaries. Taken together, these factors suggest a compelling economic logic to war in Sri Lanka.

WHAT ACCOUNTS FOR THE 2002 CEASEFIRE?

---

[76] Celia W. Dugger, "Army cash props up Sri Lanka," *Taipei Times* (20 August 2001),
also see the weekly 'Situation Report' column by Iqbal Aththas in *The Sunday Times*
(Colombo).
[77] Mick Moore, "Leading the Left to the Right: Populist Coalitions and Economic
Reform," in *World Development* 25, no. 7 (1997), 1009-1028.

The signing of an indefinite ceasefire between the Sri Lankan government and the LTTE in February 2002 poses a seemingly awkward question of the current analysis. Why, if the economic logic underpinning war in Sri Lanka has been so strong, have there been moves to end hostilities? The answer, it is suggested here, lies in two key factors; that war was no longer financially sustainable for the Sri Lankan government[78] and that important stakeholders, notably domestic capital, were no longer willing to tolerate the pursuit of war.

Perhaps the most obvious link between the economy and peace is the worsening economic conditions experienced in the year or so leading up to the signing of the ceasefire. Sri Lanka's GDP fell by 1.4 per cent over calendar year 2001, the first ever contraction since the country gained independence in 1948. The slowdown can be attributed to several factors that underline the internationalisation of Sri Lanka's economy. Being linked to the global economy, Sri Lanka suffered the adverse effects of worldwide economic slowdown during 2001. Low export earnings from the primary commodities sector, falling levels of FDI in each of the four years to 2001 (Table 1), and shrinking development assistance made things worse. International financial institutions and donors had long been calling for further reform of the Sri Lankan economy and had, since a joint meeting in Paris in December 2000, taken the position that aid would be reduced dramatically unless there was progress on both peace and economic reform.[79] As a result of these factors, the government's fiscal future was also looking dire – government deficits were growing and military expenditure was consistently overrunning budget allocations, especially during the costly Elephant Pass cam-

---

[78] The economic imperatives that may have acted on the LTTE are more difficult to establish. It is often suggested that the LTTE was experiencing difficulties in fundraising amongst the Tamil Diaspora because several countries in which Tamils had settled had proscribed the LTTE during the late 1990s. The situation is said to have been made more difficult for the LTTE by the US-led 'war on terror' launched after the events of 11 September 2001. These financial limits and geo-political pressures may go some way in explaining why the LTTE was prepared to sign a ceasefire agreement.

[79] See Mieko Nishimizu's concluding remarks from that meeting. Also, according to Richard Armitage the then US Deputy Secretary of State, 'Just a few years ago, the United States was considering discontinuing our development assistance program to Sri Lanka, given the on-going conflict' (Statement at the Tokyo donour conference, 9 June 2003).

paign of early 2000. It was clear that the government could ill-afford to pursue its increasingly costly military strategy without further increasing the tax burden or government debt or both.

There were also indications during the late 1990s that the LTTE was increasingly prepared to launch attacks on key economic targets outside the Northeast.[80] The most devastating of these attacks was carried out in July 2001 on the island's only international airport and resulted in the destruction of several air force and civilian aircraft. This was followed in October 2001 by the sinking of an oil tanker off the coast. After the airport attack the LTTE leader is said to have issued a public warning that there would be more attacks on economic targets.[81] Importantly, the attack on the airport challenged, for the first time, the fundamental mechanisms that supported the economy. At one level, the attack threatened the global linkages that have been important engines of Sri Lankan growth. Tourist arrivals fell dramatically and the higher insurance levies on air and sea craft visiting Sri Lanka increased export costs. At another level, the disruption to insurance markets and risk management, key factors in the ability of an economy to balance temporal uncertainty, represented a far more serious threat to economic well-being than previous incidents. Finally, the geographical isolation of the fighting to the Northeast that had hitherto allowed the rest of the island's economy to grow could no longer be assured.

Meanwhile, the government's strategy of favouring recurrent expenditure over capital expenditure[82] was also starting to take its toll on the economic fundamentals. Under pressure to finance military expenditure but also to keep budget deficits down, successive governments had under-invested in non-military economic services.[83] Key infrastructure was inadequate and/or badly depleted. The cost to the economy of reduced public investment is estimated to have been

---

[80] This includes attacks on several oil depots in 1995, on the Central Bank in 1996, and on Colombo's World Trade Centre in 1997.

[81] "Tigers in massive recruitment drive using video of airport attack" in *The Island* (2 September 2001).

[82] Dunham and Kelegama, *op.cit.*, 1997, 183.

[83] Grobar and Gnanaselvam, *op.cit.*, 1993; Arunatilake, Jayasuriya, and Kelegama, *op.cit.*, 2001, 1491; and Sarvananthan, *op.cit.*, 2002.

at least US$500 million.[84] Similarly, the manufacturing sector had received no large-scale public investment and very little private investment.[85]

Sri Lanka's fledgling stock market, which had grown despite hostilities in the early 1990s, had been losing value since the late 1990s. A happy coincidence of the end of first Gulf War, high real domestic interest rates and a second wave of liberalisation (including of exchange controls) attracted considerable foreign investor interest, especially from investors looking to tap into 'emerging markets.' Driven by strong foreign interest, the All Share Price Index (ASPI) of the Colombo Stock Exchange (CSE) increased by more than 60 per cent in calendar year 1993, said to have been the highest growth at any exchange in the world that year.[86] However, from that peak, the ASPI fell on an almost annual basis for the rest of the decade to less than half of its 1993 value in 2000, with foreign investors being net sellers from 1998-2001. All but a few major investors (for example, Japan's NTT in the telecommunications sector and Emirates in the airline sector) had been scared off by years of war and insecurity.

It was perhaps not surprising then that the most powerful peace lobby to emerge in late 2001 was a group of domestic business leaders under the banner of 'Sri Lanka First.' This was one of the most concerted and organised pressure groups calling for peace in recent Sri Lankan history.[87] Domestic business was suffering not just because of the economic downturn, but also from years of under-investment and the retreat of international investors. While the rural poor may have escaped the worst effects of the war, for domestic capital the war was starting to cost too much. Any goodwill established between business elites and political elites of the ruling Sri Lanka Freedom Party (SLFP) was being withered away. Despite winning Presidential elections in December 2000, economic stagnation and the loss of international support were instrumental in the defeat of the SLFP-led government in the general elections in December

---

[84] Arunatilake, Jayasuriya, and Kelegama, *op.cit.*, 2001, 1492.
[85] Moore, *op.cit.*, 1990. 354-5.
[86] See CSE Information Resources, accessed online at www.cse.lk/about_cse/ inforesources.jsp; also see Amita Shastri, "Transitions to a free market: Economic Liberalisation in Sri Lanka," in *The Round Table* 344 (1997), 485-511&485.
[87] Feizal Samath, *Business: Better Late than Never* (Colombo: IPS, 2002).

2001. In contrast, building on the work of groups such as 'Sri Lanka First,' the pro-business UNP-led coalition successfully linked renewed economic growth and political settlement with LTTE in its election manifesto. As the victorious Sri Lankan Prime Minister declared, 'business is good for peace and peace is good for business.'[88]

What emerged in aftermath of the signing of the ceasefire was confirmation of the shared economic priorities of the major stakeholders – a phenomenon termed elsewhere as the 'Killinochchi consensus.'[89] While critical negotiations on military and political issues stalled – and remain stalled – there was early progress in delivering an economic 'peace dividend.' The government, LTTE, international donors and the business sector shared a common strategy of pursuing peace building *through* economic development. As economic circumstances changed, so too did the strategies of key players. Now economic factors were driving towards peace.

CONCLUSION

At the time of writing, a permanent settlement to the Sri Lankan conflict seems as elusive as ever. This elusiveness of peace is a testament to the complexity of the Sri Lankan case and also a reminder that any analysis of it has to be sufficiently nuanced. Accordingly, the aim of this article has not been to suggest the operation of a simplistic economic determinism. Rather, it has been to flag important aspects of understanding conflict in Sri Lanka and to restate the importance of economic factors in developing that understanding. With this in mind, it is perhaps useful to turn to what lessons a political economy of sri lanka's conflict might hold for efforts to secure that elusive peace.

First, this exploration of the nexus between economics and conflict has highlighted the need to see the conflict in Sri Lanka as the product of both political factors (for example, ethno-political mobilisation) and economic strategies (for example, rent-seeking).

---

[88] Ranil Wickremesinghe, Address by Prime Minister at the "Investing in Peace" in New York City, 19 September 2002 reported in *The Island* (22 September 2002).

[89] Dhananjayan Sriskandarajah, "The returns of peace in Sri Lanka: the development cart before the conflict resolution horse?" in *Journal of Peacebuilding and Development*, 1, no. 2 (2003); also available as a monograph published by the International Centre for Ethnic Studies (ICES), Colombo.

Understanding the interaction between economic change and political conflict strikes at the heart of economic theorising. Part of the problem is that war blurs the distinction between (economically) productive and (physically) destructive activities. War and peace emerge as alternative politico-military strategies whose pursuit is conditional, at least in part, on the prevailing economic imperatives of key stakeholders. Predicting which strategies and processes will be conflict-generating or conflict-ameliorating is difficult but important. This is especially true when we see that 'ethnic' groups do not have homogeneous economic interests. Rather, important differences in economic agendas within and between groups can drive political agendas. From a peace building perspective, it is important to note that if key stakeholders see sufficient gain from resumed war with the knowledge that they can insulate themselves from the adverse impacts of that war, and if key protagonists can once again find the wherewithal to fight a war, then the chances of a resumption of hostilities are high.

Secondly, it is clear that economic factors are important amongst the generative structures, mechanisms and forces that have shaped the dynamics of the ethno-political conflict in Sri Lanka. There was an outbreak of hostilities during a period of economic uncertainty, those hostilities were transformed into war during a period of relatively high economic growth, and there has been a move towards peace at a time of economic contraction. Understanding these linkages between material conditions and political crises is critical to the historiography of Sri Lanka's conflict and also to understanding what levers might be deployed to further peace in the future.

Thirdly, this article has tried to highlight the importance of spatial factors in shaping the dynamics of Sri Lanka's conflict, not just in terms of where hostilities occurred but also in terms of economic and political governance. Sri Lanka's wartime economy can perhaps be best understood as being made up of three distinct spatial components: a fast-growing, export-oriented zone around Colombo; a rural Southwest being carried along; and a war-torn Northeast. The physical, economic and political interaction of these regions has had a profound influence on the dynamics of the ethno-political conflict in Sri Lanka. Further, as Gunasinghe and others have pointed out, the contradictions of economic liberalisation and the emergence of supra-national economic governance are implicated in Sri Lanka's 'ethnic' conflict. Just as national economic space has become harder to manage during the period of globalisation, so too have the spatial dimensions of 'internal' conflicts. The internationalisation of Sri Lanka's conflict, through the movement of people, ideologies and finance, has meant that Sri Lanka's conflict is only a 'civil war' in name. This internationalisation aided the military effort of the major protagonists but international involvement was also critical in securing the 2002 ceasefire. The importance of that political, economic and perhaps military involvement is unlikely to diminish.

A robust political economy of an ethno-political economy must also engage with broader issues such as the formation and deployment of identities (groupings); the articulation of material and discursive strategies; perceptions and aspirations about greed, grievance, and the apportionment of blame; and the very issue of individual agency in the face of assumed collective allegiances. Most of all, such a framework must, as Gunasinghe aimed to do, interrogate the 'linkages between economic structure and ethnic contradictions.'

Dhananjayan Sriskandarajah *is a doctoral candidate in the School of Geography, University of Oxford, UK working on the political economy of conflict in multi-ethnic developing countries.*

In our regular re-publication, *'Domains* Recollects' we
feature Radhika Coomaraswamy's 2001 address to the
University of Melbourne School of Law, which is not
widely available in print in the US or Sri Lanka.

Broken Glass: Women, Violence and the Rule of Law

Radhika Coomaraswamy

I was recently in Sierra Leone on mission for the United Nations when the representative of the Office of The High Commissioner for Human Rights introduced me to the team that was in
charge of The Rule of Law project. When I asked them to explain
their work, they spoke of advancing law reform that would ensure
accountability and the protection of human rights. They also enu-
merated plans for the training of judges and public prosecutors so as
to make them sensitive to the due process of law. They also outlined
projects of working with the police to ensure that the police would
implement the law respecting the rights and privileges of citizens.
When I was in Cambodia a few year earlier I was introduced to 'The
Rule of Law' project there which included as a high priority the
building of prisons so that perpetrators were not immediately executed but were given a fair trial and humane punishment. In East
Timor, Kosovo and other areas where the United Nations is present
in full force as supposed trustees of world civilization, the projects
on The Rule of Law are important components of their day to day
activities. The concept of the Rule of Law has been greatly trans-

formed from the narrow, limited sense first articulated by Dicey.[1] For Dicey, The Rule of Law had three components. The first was that individuals should not be subject to the arbitrary, wide discretionary powers of those in government and that such discretion should be limited by a regime of laws and rules. The second component was that all subjects are equal before the law and no-one should be singled out or privileged under a system that was true to the Rule of Law. And finally he argued that the Rule of Law ultimately rested with the judiciary that would determine individual cases based on time-honoured principles. For Dicey and for many of us schooled in the Anglo American system of law, the rule of law was about the primacy of principles over personalities, about equality and about an independent and powerful judiciary.

However, today in the world of international jurisprudence, the concept of *The Rule of Law* has moved beyond its origins in Dicey and The Anglo American legal reality. The Rule of Law as put forward by UN agencies and other donors is more akin to Michel Foucault's view of what he termed The Enlightenment project.[2] For Foucault, the western Enlightenment brought with it certain discourses and technologies of power that through colonialism and its aftermath continue to dominate the world of ideas. For Foucault and French post-structuralists, there are no universal truths, or ideas that are essential through time. Truth and knowledge are contingent, historical and rooted in a dynamic of power. The discourse and technologies of The Enlightenment supported by a Kantian metaphysiscs give a sense that there are universal truths and eternal principles. In analysing these principles in the realm of justice and punishment in his book *Discipline and Punish*, Foucault shows how new notions of humanity, discipline and surveillance gained currency in the western world in the eighteenth and nineteenth century.[3] For example, in the past, those who fell afoul of those in power were punished in public, their bodies tortured and destroyed, today in the post-enlightenment

---

[1] A.V. Dicey, *Introduction to the Study of the Law of the Constitution*, ([1885] 10th Edition (ed.) E.C.S. Wade, (London: Macmillan, 1958)).
[2] Christopher Norris, "What is Enlightenment: Kant and Foucault" in Gary Gutting (ed.), *The Cambridge Companion to Foucault*, (Cambridge: The University Press, 1994).

era, in Cambodia and elsewhere, we build prisons so that prisoners may be disciplined and rehabilitated according to the dictates of the new humanism.

The United Nations has now been entrusted with taking the Enlightenment project to the peripheral territories of world civilisation in the guise of The Rule of Law project. Institutions such as representative government, an independent judiciary, a human rights sensitive police force and prisons with rehabilitation as their main fopus are being fostered, funded and implemented by UN agencies and donor countries. This is not necessarily a bad thing. Often the alternative is summary execution, torture, arbitrary power or violence. For those of us schooled in the latter half of the twentieth century, The Enlightenment project, which according to Foucault includes both liberalism and Marxism, is still superior to what went before it. However, Foucault's writings are a warning that The Rule of Law, despite its pretensions of objectivity and neutrality, is, in the final analysis, also a system of power. It includes and excludes people, it disciplines and punishes and it fosters certain values and attitudes encasing them in a belief that they are time-honoured and eternal.

Modern day feminism owes a great deal to thinkers such as Michel Foucault. As Jana Sawicki writes, "Foucault brings to our attention historical transformations...in order to reveal their contingency and to free us for new possibilities of self understanding, new modes of experience, new forms of subjectivity, authority and political identity."[4] In preparing for this lecture, I wondered what would be a feminist analysis of the Rule of Law in light of the data and evidence I have gathered as Special Rapporteur on Violence Against Women. Feminism means different things to different people. For sensational, polemical outsiders it is sometimes seen as a radical, man hating ideology. For more discerning minds, interested in social justice, feminism is seen as the attempt to fight for equality between the sexes in public and private spaces as well as an attempt to make women's experiences, long ignored in the public sphere, a legitimate

[3] Michel Foucault, *Discipline and Punish: The Birth of the Prison*, (tran.) Alan Sheridon, (New York: Vintage, 1985).
[4] Jana Sawicki, "Foucault, Feminism and Questions of Identity" in Gutting (ed.), *op. cit.*, 288.

aspect of decisionmaking and authority. But for feminist academics, feminism is not only about the achievement of discernible goals. It is also about process and method. Gananath Obeyesekere, in a recent lecture in Sri Lanka, argued that the nineteenth century produced three great thinkers who were extraordinary because they were the "masters of suspicion." These thinkers were Marx, Nietzsche and Freud. These great thinkers were very suspicious of the world as it appeared. They challenged prevailing orthodoxies and looked for other motivations that drove individuals and collectivities. Whether it is the mode of production, the inner psyche of the mind or the will to power they gave us valuable insights into society as it actually exists as opposed to how it appears to exist. Most of all they gave us methodologies for criticism and critical inquiry, what Michel Foucault has argued was the single greatest contribution of The Enlightenment. Some of us see feminism as being part of that tradition, as a mistress of suspicion, as a vantage point to critique and analyse what exists, with the hope of moving fonyard in the'future to a more egalitarian and empowering society for all human beings.

What then would be a feminist critique of The Rule of Law doctrine in its broadest sense. There are many areas to this inquiry, many avenues for reflection. I am going to focus on three aspects- the first aspect will deal with the boundaries of the rule of law and the denial of women's concerns; the second aspect will look at certain values and attitudes contained fostered by The Rule of Law and its implications for the rights of women. The third aspect will speak to the type of human personality celebrated by The Rule of Law and the reality of women's experience.

It is often said that the quality of a system of laws may be better understood by analysing its effects on society's margins. This involves questions such as who is included in the law's protection? Who is excluded? Who is privileged? Who is actually punished?- these questions give a sense of the social dimension of a legal system as it actually affects people's lives. The Rule of Law as a legal construct is meant to ensure a measure of process, fairness and transparency for individuals in society. It allows for the accountability of those who transgress the law by invoking objective, neutral principles administered by independent judges. It opens individual transgressions to public scrutiny and judgment. However, it may be

# # # # #

argued that the full protection of The Rule of Law is only available in the public sphere where men dominate and live out their daily lives. In most societies around the world, the family is private space. For the most part, it is space away from public judgment, an inchoate contingent space that is generally not defined by strict rules and their enforcement. It is protected space, away from the gaze of the state. As Debra Morris writes, privacy is "a special kind of reprieve from social control."[5] It is transitional space where we suspend judgment of others, decline to get involved and allow people to be themselves. However, for many feminists this private space has been a historical site for the abuse of women by men without public scrutiny or the Rule of Law. The reprieve that The Rule of Law gives to the private has allowed for domestic violence, incest and child abuse to exist without state interference or action. The violence against women movement of the 1980s was a desperate attempt to bring public scrutiny, the Rule of Law and human rights, into the private domain so that violent abuse of women and children would cease. The self-imposed boundaries of The Rule of Law construct that prevents it from entering the domain of the private were seriously , I challenged as part of the patriarchal foundations of the legal system.[6] Twenty years of activism in this area has clearly shown for example in Brazil, that violence against women in the home is rarely acknowledged and if acknowledged rarely provided with redress.[7] The strong movement against violence against women in Latin America demanded that the private be subject to The Rule of Law, that husbands who commit violence against their wives be given the same criminal treatment as those that commit violence against strangers. The furor against the inability of the law or the criminal justice system to respond to widespread violence against women resulted in the

[5] Debra Morris, "Privacy, Privation, Perversity: Toward New Representations of the Personal" in *Signs: Journal of Women in Culture and Society* (2000) 25, no. 2, 325.
[6] For example at the international level see Celina Romany "State Responsibility Goes Private: A Feminist Critique of the Public/Private Distinction in International Human Rights Law" in Rebecca J. Cook (ed.) *Human Rights of Women: National and International Perspectives* (Pennsylvania Studies in Human Rights) (Philadelphia: University of Pennsylvania Press, 1994).
[7] See Human Rights Watch, *Criminal Injustice: Violence Against Women in Brazil*, (New York: Human Rights Watch, 1991).

creation of special police stations for women in Brazil that would specialize in domestic violence cases.

Some of the renowned feminists of the 70s and 80s such as Catherine Mackinnon made their name by arguing that the private was a deeply political space where male domination was sanctified. By calling domestic violence a form of torture, they sought maximum public scrutiny for violence in the home.[8] Of all existing human rights norms, torture is the most widely accepted doctrine, recognized as *jus cogens*, a principle of international law that cannot be derogated from. When writers such as Rhonda Copeland defined domestic violence as torture, they did so to force open the construction of the private and to subject it to the most rigorous form of public accountability.[9]

Male violence against women and children under the cover of the private has an extraordinary history throughout the world. Such violence is usually beyond the Rule of Law and even if it is illegal on paper, in actual practice, criminal justice systems are usually insensitive or oblivious. Recently there has been a great deal of discussion involving crimes of honour and the inability of states to take action against such crimes. In many societies, especially in West Asia and some countries in Latin America men kill the women in their families for violations of "the family honour" and are never punished. In some countries, honour is a legitimate defense, even for a murder charge. In other countries, even if the formal legal system does not recognize an honor defense, in cases involving honor, the police will not arrest, the prosecutors will not file charges and judges and juries are ready to acquit. As a result perpetrators go free.[10]

Crimes of honor vary with each culture. For some it involves cases where women commit - adultery and are subject to wife murder by their husbands. In other countries, the crimes of honor may involve women falling in love with the wrong person, wanting a divorce, wanting to choose their own marriage partner and sometimes

---

[8] Catherine MacKinnon, "On Torture: A Feminist Perspective on Human Rights," in (ed.) Kathleen Mahoney, *Human Rights in the Twenty First Century: A Global Challenge* (New York: Springer, 1994).

[9] Rhonda Copeland, "Intimate Terror: Understanding Domestic Violence As Torture" in (ed.) Cook, *op. cit.*, 1994.

[10] Human Rights Watch, *op.cit.*, 1991.

even being a victim of rape.[11] Fathers, brothers and husbands kill the women in their family for even these seemingly trivial transgressions. In some communities, the men stone to death the family member in front of the community. It is not only men that sanction this kind of activity. Mothers of honor crime victims, when-interviewed in Pakistan, were fully supportive of the men in their families. To a woman they would argue that the victim "deserved it."[12]

It is not only in countries in the third world where the "oriental other" is located that such crimes of honour are recognized. Feminists analysing the defense of provocation in western legal systems have found that it has been used to free many husbands who have killed their wives but is not 'as easily available for wives who kill their husbands. In most societies there is an acceptance of the proposition that if a wife acts in a manner that brings shame on her husband, violence against her can be understood, if not justified. The, reverse is of course not the case.[13] In very few societies is a woman's wrath at her husband shaming her ever tolerated.

What is the root cause of this concept of honour, which regulates codes of conduct in many societies and which, is often beyond the Rule of Law. A sociologist would probably argue that a great deal of honour related activity is linked to the control of - female sexuality. Others would add that this control of sexuality is an attempt to ensure that property passes to the 'rightful heirs" and that women's freedom is curtailed so that only so called legitimate children will receive the fruits of a husband's labour.[14] But there is also something more; something less describable, less clear-cut in its answer. The anthropologist Gananath Obeyesekere has argued that many societies are motivated by what he calls in Sinhalese *Lajja/Bhaya-* fear and shame.[15] Fear and shame and fear of " shame have motivated people to commit horrendous acts in peace and at

---

[11] Leyla Pervizat, *Report to The Special Rapporteur on Violence Against Women on Honour Crimes in Turkey*, 1999

[12] Amnesty International, *Pakistan: Violence Against Women in The Name of Honour*, 1999.

[13] Human Rights Watch, *Global Report of Women's Human Rights*, (New York, Human Rights Watch, 1995), 363

[14] Patrica Uberoi, (ed.) *Social Reform, Sexuality and the State* (Delhi, Sage, 1996).

[15] Gananath Obeyesekere, *Medusa's Hair: An Essay on Personal Symbols and Religious Experience*, (Chicago: University of Chicago Press, 1981).

war. Honor is . said to be linked to a person's sense of public esteem. To attack that esteem is a terrible crime in most societies. That is why the honor defense is seen as an aspect of self-defense and justified in terms of self-defense. The tragedy of honor crimes is that a woman's emotional and sexual behaviour is seen to have a direct reflection on her husband's, or a family's sense of public esteem. Her transgressions are evidence that he cannot control her and the inability of a man to control his woman is to bring him directly into public disrepute. In some sense he owns her behaviour and his public persona is implicitly conditioned by her obedience. I remember a Sri Lankan astrologer telling my mother with horror in his eyes, "You will have a willful daughter" as if willful daughters were a fate worse than death. Honor then is directly linked to a denial of woman's freedom and women's autonomy. Societies often seem ill at ease with a woman's right to choose.

It is not only crimes of violence that interrogate our constructions of the private, it is also the conduct of family life. In 1979,The International Convention on The Elimination of - All Forms of Discrimination (CEDAW) came into being. Next to The Convention on The Rights of the Child, it is the most ratified Convention in international legal history although many countries have introduced reservations when signing it.[16] Article 16 of CEDAW has detailed provisions outlining the fact that free and full consent and equality between spouses before, during and after marriage should be enshrined in law. In actual fact, throughout the world there are a plethora of laws governing private life, the vast majority of which flagrantly violate Article 16 of CEDAW. Women are subject to unequal inheritance, they are denied free and full consent at the time of marriage, they may have to experience polygamy, unilateral divorce, discrimination in child custody provisions and they may even be married off as children. However, whenever women in these countries attempt to bring forward some sort of egalitarian regime, they are viciously attacked for trying to destroy the culture of the society. So while the society at large discovers the internet, the free market and representative democracy, any attempt to change family laws and personal laws is seen as a pernicious attempt by the west and western agents to destroy the culture of the society. It is in family life then that culture is preserved; it is family law that must remain impervious to change.

How do these plethora of family laws implicate the concept of The Rule Of Law? One of Dicey's basic principles was that there should be equality before the law, that similar categories should be given similar treatment. However, in many countries women are not - equal to each other. The most important aspect of most women's lives is the family and the rights and responsibilities with regard to family life differ according to which ethnic group or religious minority women belong to. In Sri Lanka, Muslim women have different rights from Tamil women and Tamil women from Kandyan Sinhalese women. Their fundamental right to equality as women is compromised in favour of the preservation of cultural relativism in family life.

Partha Chatterjee[17] in an important article on Indian nationalism argues that sometime by the mid nineteen twenties, there was an implicit understanding among Indian nationalists about how they would deal with western influence and the modern world. Again the world would be divided into the public and the private. Men would dominate the public world that would rely on western models of the market, socialism and representative democracy. The public would be implicated in India's drive to become a modern powerful nation and would draw heavily from the ideologies and technologies of modernity. However, women would dominate the private space and it would be the space where a society's culture and tradition are preserved in rituals and practices of the household. The private would be the spiritual space where Indianness would find expression. Women would become the primary figures in cultural preservation and reproduction.

---

[16] For a detailed account see Rebecca Cook, "State Accountability Under the Convention on the Elimination of All Forms of Discrimination Against Women" in (ed.) Cook, op. cit., 1994, 228

[17] Partha Chatterjee, "The Nationalist Resolution of the Women's Question" in (eds.) Kumkum Sangari and Sudesh Vaid, *Recasting Women: Essays in Colonial History*, (Delhi, Kali for Women, 1989).

In many ways, the same compromise has been reached with many other ethnic groups. Except for the Taliban in Afghanistan and perhaps a few other societies, most other countries have accepted the modern as the most dominant way of "being" in the public world. The internet, the market, contemporary technology, industrial development and modern forms of agro economics are adopted throughout the world. However, family life and women's roles are still seen as essential for the preservation of Sri Lankan culture. Any suggestion that the personal, family laws of ethnic groups be changed to suit modern needs is met with vicious antagonism. The situation is made worse by the fact that chauvinist elements within majorities and dominant groups are quick to support causes that want to eradicate the cultural laws of minorities. Scholars and activists arguing for pluralism and respect for diversity are often very critical of feminists for being in open alliance with racists and fundamentalists who want to deny the plural and diverse nature of many Asian and African societies.

This desire to respect diversity and the lifestyles of different ethnic groups is an important part of the modern struggle against racism. Therefore it is very important that women win their rights without accentuating general intolerance and contempt for diverse ethnic groups. This struggle for women's rights is also about the struggle for dignity. For many women, their sense of dignity often comes from how their ethnic group is treated in the wider community. For women's rights activists to attack minority cultures frontally is to assault other aspects of a woman's sense of self. For this reason, fearing a partnership with rightwing Hindu nationalist groups, the women's movement in India has basically given up the call for The Uniform Civil Code that treats all women equally.[18] Right wing Hindu groups had taken up the call for a Uniform Code so as to remove Muslim law from the law books. Muslim women and women's activists would thereby become unwilling agents in the greater marginalisation of the Muslim community.

In trying to deal with the issue of equality and the universality of human rights while respecting cultural diversity in the law,

---

[18] See Brenda Cossman and Ratna Kapur, *Subversive Sites: Feminist Engagements With Law in India*, (Delhi: Sage, 1996), Chapter 4.

South Africa has come up with an innovative solution with regard to the diverse customary laws relating to family relations in their country.[19] The South African Law Commission attempted to reconcile these positions by receiving communications and speaking with experts. Finally they formulated two elements that should create the framework for reconciling universality with diversity. First, every couple should be given the option as to whether they would be governed by the customary law or the general law that is consistent with South Africa's obligations under CEDAW. Second, despite the optionality, all diverse customary laws must have a minimum core of provisions that relate to women's rights. These generally relate to a woman's free and full consent to enter the marriage and during the marriage as well as her economic protection during marriage and when the marriage is over due to death or dissolution. Strangely, The Commission did not focus on strict equality. They permitted practices such as *lobolo-* bride practice- and polygamy if the woman involves consents to the practice.

What they attempted to preserve was woman's autonomy and her ability to make decisions with regard to her marriage. For example a man is allowed to take a second wife only after he has entered into an agreement with his first wife about her. maintenance and property and after receiving her consent. Both the provision on optionality as well as that which stresses the minimum core principle recognize that women may wish to participate in their culture as its exists. However, they place great emphasis on a woman's right to choose and create structures and processes that allow her to make realistic decisions about her life.

The South African Law Commission approach is then an attempt to bring the principles associated with the Rule of Law, principles of fairness and equality, into the private sphere while being sensitive to other societal needs. Feminists have waged a very strong struggle to subject the private to a strict enforcement of the law. The campaign against domestic violence has been one of the main factors in this desire to pry open the private to the public gaze. However, in recent times, there have been other voices that argue that we should

---

[19] For an interesting article on the process see David Chambers, "Civilizing The Natives: Marriage in Post Apartheid South Africa" in *Daedalus* (Fall 2000), 10

reclaim the private, that the rule of law should not intrude into our intimate lives and that we must construct new notions of the private that are not subject to violence or abuse.

As many feminists have claimed, there is no place where power does not operate. However, as legal philosopher Patricia Williams has argued, there must still be a space in our lives where we have a "reprieve" from the politics of power and the surveillance associated with public judgment.[20] There must be a space for "the intractable, the incongruous, the incommensurate;"[21] a place for mystery, for intimacy, for fantasy. We must be able to exist somewhere free from constant scrutiny and constant accountability. There must be spaces where we can hide our vulnerability. The struggle against totalitarian regimes is after all partly about the preservation of those spaces. It is therefore extremely interesting to read some of the new writing about women and women's rights that is trying to recover the private in a meaningful way. Arguing that the earlier feminist debate and the existing legal systems are based on a false dichotomy between private and public, they suggest alternative ways of looking at the social. They offer theoretical insights on how privacy can be reinvented so as to deny abuse and violence while protecting and having "regard for another's fragile, mysterious autonomy."[22] The conversation is just beginning among young, dynamic scholars. Many of us interested in modern ideas of jurisprudence must surely begin to explore how legal structures and " principles can react to this recovery of the private in what will be a new era. While the boundaries of The Rule of Law clearly present dilemmas for those of us interested in women's rights, it is also important to acknowledge that the law fosters ideas and attitudes that condition the way women live and behave in any given society. Dicey's concept of The Rule of Law is a procedural one that aims at being value free, focusing on process and method. However, Foucault's notion of The Rule of Law is premised on the fact that such a construct is full of attitudes, biases and prejudice, requiring in his words a science of archeology, to excavate the layers of formal and

---

[20] Patricia Williams, *The Alchemy of Race and Rights* (Cambridge, MA.: Harvard University Press, 1991).
[21] Debra Morris, *op. cit.*, 330.
[22] Williams, *op. cit.*, 164.

informal discourse. One cannot explore all dimensions in the course of one lecture but, as United Nations Special Rapporteur on Violence Against Women, I have found the law's attitude to female sexuality a great area of great interest arid controversy. It conditions the laws of rape, prostitution and trafficking, sexual harassment and pornography- practically all the topics that are within my mandate. With regard to rape, societies attempt to regulate nonconsensual sex between individuals through the laws of rape. The formal law approaches female sexuality from the vantage point of the construction of the word "consent." Rape is often defined as intercourse or sexual assault that is committed without the consent of the woman concerned. In a recent survey of rape laws around the world, The International Criminal Tribunal for The Former Yugoslavia found that this is the common factor in all rape laws around the world and across all legal systems. However, the more interesting aspect is how the word; consent is interpreted and constructed.[23] In many countries women have to physically resist and have near death experiences to show that they did not consent.[24] In earlier centuries and in some countries today, the issue is not even one of resistance, if a woman is seen as "unchaste," or "unrespectable"[25] she is deemed to have consented. In addition, analysing rape cases, scholars have found that many of them rest on scrutinising the conduct of the victim not of the defendant.[26] In fact some scholars argue that the rape trial was often turned into a pornographic spectacle and performed that function in earlier centuries?[27] Feminists studying these issues have found that there is an actual hierarchy with regard to the rape victims. If one is young and a virgin, one is far more likely to receive justice than if one were middle-aged and married.[28] For the legal system, as it actually operates, the sexuality of a virgin is far more precious than the sexuality of a more mature woman. In many societies a woman's past sexual history can still be introduced into evidence even if it has

---

[23] See Carol Smart, *Feminism and the Power of the Law,* (New York: Routledge, 1989), 34-43.
[24] See Susan Estrich, "Rape," in *The Yale Law Journal*, 95, 1087.
[25] Carol Smart, *op. cit.*, 41-44
[26] Susan Estrich, *op. cit.*, 1094.
[27] Smart, op. cit., 41-43.
[28] Catherine MacKinnon "Reflections on Sex Equality Under Law," 100 *The Yale Law Journal*, 100, 1281, 1304-1307.

nothing to do with the facts of the case. Secondly, research into the issues of rape and race in the United States shows clearly how rape of white women by black men would result in fierce, instant justice, rape of white women by white men, some justice but rape of black women by black women is usually ignored. The rape of Black women by White men is not even talked about. In fact, powerful Black women writers have argued how the hidden history of slavery rests on the sexual exploitation of black women.[29]

Sexuality is therefore not only the site of rape of women by men but it is also the location where race relations are often played out in many societies. Research into cases of the lynching of Black men by white mobs on allegations of rape has given the charge of rape a disturbing history in the United States of America.[30] Coetze's Booker prize novel of last year *Disgrace*[31] tells a story of inter-racial rape in post apartheid South Africa, a story so painful to read because of the actual history of race relations in that country. For women's activists who see rape as the most heinous crime, it is no great comfort to see black man after black man go to jail while other perpetrators go free. Do we ask for more draconian laws on rape when we know that in the present context it will be applied to put men from marginalized communities in jail. Through the offense of rape, the law polices nonconsensual sex. However this policing does not take place in a power vacuum and continues to pose great dilemmas especially in terms of the law's application. While the field of rape conjures up the image of a young innocent virgin becoming a victim to unbridled male sexuality, other areas of the law produce a different picture of women. Many scholars have argued that in the Christian world, religious and legal systems live in fear of female sexual agency. As Efrat Ttseelon writes "through Eve the original sin becomes sexualized and demonized. Her temptation to eat the forbidden fruit becomes seduction, and the seducer-the serpent- a de-

---

[29] bell hooks, *Ain't I a Woman: Black Women and Feminism* (Boston: South End Press, 1981).
[30] For a lucid analysis see Kimberle Crenshaw, "Whose life is it Anyway? Feminist and Antiracist Appropriations of Anita Hill" in Toni Morrison (ed.) *Race-ing Justice, En-Gendering Power : Essays on Anita Hill, Clarence Thomas, and the Construction of Social Reality* (New York: Pantheon, 1992).
[31] J. M. Coetze, *Disgrace*, (New York: Vintage, 2000).

monic infusion between evil and sexuality."[32] Recently Uma Chack-ravarti, a leading Indian historian analysed legal approaches to sexu-ality in pre-colonial Maharashthra in India. In Hindu lives, the married ; woman with children was valorized and glorified. As a re-sult women outside that framework were debased, especially widows who were subject to the most terrible indignities if they did not im-molate themselves on their husband's pyre.[33] Again Chackravarti ar-gues, fear of female sexuality that was not harnessed to a specific man made the laws ruthless toward unmarried women, widows, and women who committed adultery. In Africa, a Woman Minister en-treated The Office of The Special Rapporteur on Violence Against Women not to make a fuss about female circumcision. She was very clear that circumcision was the only way to keep women "modest" and "chaste," without "giving into their desires." To attack the prac-tice was to attack the heart of the society's culture.

This notion that women as active sexual agents will make men go haywire is at the root of many legal systems in their stric-tures about family morality. Today a great deal of attention has been focused on the Muslim world where the Taliban continue to generate caricature images of a complex and diverse community. Women are subject to dress codes, women are not allowed in public without a *Bourqua*, women are not allowed education or employment oppor-tunities and adultery or fornication will result in public lashing.[34] According to Pinar Ilkkaracan who has done a detailed study of sexuality in Muslim societies, all these taboos are in some part a re-sult of male fears of unbridled female sexuality. Drawing from the scriptures, she shows how women are described as sexually potent individuals who must be resisted. Before we give into the instinct of making the Muslim community into the "Oriental Other" it may be interesting to note that just a century ago in England writers such as Tertullianus were arguing that women should be veiled. These church fathers wrote that women who went to public baths "prostitute to

---

[32] Efrat Tseelon, *The Masque of Femininity : The Presentation of Woman in Every-day Life*, (London, Sage, 1995).

[33] Uma Chakravarti, in Uberoi, *op.cit.*, 1996.

[34] For a fuller description see Report of The Special Rapporteur on Violence Against Women, Mission to Pakistan and Afghanistan, Commission on Human Rights Doc E/CN.4/2000/6.8/ Add.4 (2000)

eyes that are curious," that "every public exposure of an honorable virgin is a suffering of rape."[35] It is therefore not unbelievable in Afghanistan, a country ruled by village level Mullahs who have opted out of twentieth century that these horrendous strictures should prevail.

The fear of female sexuality does not only operate in far away Afghanistan, now "the terrorist other." The fear of female sexuality requires societies to construct their own systems of "respectability," those codes of conduct that will ensure that women will behave properly. An analysis of Indian judgments on family law and criminal law by Brenda Cossman and Ratna Kapur[36] shows clearly that the law cherishes the respectable woman who is chaste and modest and that it has very little justice for women who do not live up to a judge's notion of respectability. Adulterous women are given severe treatment while their male counterparts are treated with leniency; and in judgment after judgment, the chaste, modest, subservient wife is given relief while any woman who shows any willful temperament is dismissed out of hand. In India at least, the old Hindu ideal of the valorized married woman continues to exist though couched in Anglo American legal language.

However, despite all these strictures based on female sexuality, feminists and women scholars are themselves deeply divided about how the law should relate to sexuality. Legal philosophy and discourse in the field of women's rights has always been dominated by Catherine Mackinnon, a Professor of Law at The University of Michigan. MacKinnon has written some of the most definitive articles on the subjugation of women. For Mackinnon, sexuality is the site of female oppression. It is in fact the central element in the struggle for women's rights. While the law in many part of the world may fear unbridled female sexuality, Mackinnon is deeply distrustful of male sexuality. For her sexual expression in the contemporary world is greatly linked to the abuse and denigration of women. As a result she has spearheaded campaigns to change the laws of Minnesota and Michigan to vindicate women's rights. She has struggled to reform the rape laws, to introduce legislation on sexual harassment and to

---

[35] Efrat Tseelon, *op. cit.*, 1995.
[36] Cossman and Kapur, *op. cit.*, 1996.

have stricter laws on pornography. In one of her best known pieces she argued "Sexuality, the, is a term of power. Gender, as socially constructed, embodies it, not the reverse... sexuality is the linchpin of gender equality."[37] For Mackinnon, the law must be an active, interventionist force, disciplining men, teaching them how to behave toward women and punishing them if they do not.

Catherine Mackinnon's unambiguous position with regard to sexuality and oppression does not always translate easily into real life experiences. This is no more apparent than in the controversy that continues to surround prostitution and trafficking in the modern world. As United Nations Special Rapporteur on Violence Against Women I made a field visit to India, Nepal and Bangladesh.[38] During the visit my team had. the opportunity to; speak to many women who had worked in prostitution. Two distinct cases remain in my mind. The first is that of a young girl from Nepal who at sixteen fell in love with a young man from the village who had gone abroad. Finally she eloped with him and he took her across the border to India to the city of Poona. In Poona she was taken to a big house and was introduced to an older Nepali lady. She noticed that some money changed hands and then her boyfriend said he had to leave for a moment. He never came back. The young girl was literally tortured into submission being subject to beatings, rape and food deprivation. She finally agreed to do sex work and was later sold to Bombay where she worked on the famous Falkland Road, guarded by bouncers, in small cubicles the size of a bed, handling about ten customers a day in appalling sanitary conditions. She was finally "rescued by a Nepali NGO called Maiti Nepal and when doctors finally had a chance to meet her, they discovered that she had AIDS. When we met her we were told that she had only a few weeks to live.

The other story provides a different picture. In the outskirts of Bombay in a small suburb, I met a group of women who were former *devadasis*, children given by the parents to the village temple for prostitution. These women had migrated to Bombay and now

---

[37] Catherine MacKinnon, "Feminism, Marxism, Method, and the State: An Agenda for Theory," in *Signs* 7 (1982) 515 (1982), 530, 533.
[38] These case studies are taken from *The Report of The Special Rapporteur on Violence Against Women, Mission to Bangladesh, Nepal and India,* a United Nations Human Rights Commission Doc E/CN.4/2001/73/Adde.2

lived in the outskirts of the city and earned their keep by being sex workers. When I asked them whether the government should set up a "rehabilitation" home to help them learn new skills so that they could move away from prostitution, they became infuriated. They said they were not in need of rehabilitation that they earned an honest wage and actually contributed to the upkeep of their parents back in the village. What they wanted most is protection from AIDS as well as schooling and benefits for their children. They seemed very offended by my patronizing ways and said quite clearly that middle class women were safe because of women like them. Like Catherine MacKinnon they had a very negative view of male sexuality and felt that they were providing a public service in keeping that sexuality under control. Historically, there have been various legal models for the regulation of prostitution. The most common model is the "moralistic" model that outlaws prostitution and which punishes the prostitute, the pimp and the client. This is found in many Catholic and Islamic countries and in some states of the United States. The second model is the international model asset out in 1949 Convention on Trafficking, which is also quite widespread. This model outlaws prostitution and trafficking but punishes only those who profit off the trade and not the prostitute herself. The third model present in many countries in Europe is the regulationist model that creates certain area zones where prostitution can take place but which is strictly regulated in terms of health and sanitary conditions as well as labour practices. The final model as put forward by many new NGO groups is the model that decriminalizes prostitution, sees prostitution as sex work and focuses on the human rights of the prostitute as a worker.

The model a society chooses to regulate prostitution is intricately linked to perceptions about sexuality. For those who are strong in their belief that all sexuality must be expressed only in the context of a legitimate nuclear family marriage, a strong criminal sanction against prostitution for deterrence as well as the reiteration of a moral norm is seen as essential. For those feminists who feel sexuality is always a site of oppression, strong laws are seen as necessary to save the victim from abuse and violence. However for those who feel that a society should be more liberal in its attitudes to sexuality, that sexuality can be expressed outside marriage and that one should not pass moral judgment, then the focus is on the rights of the sex worker, her needs and her concerns. In actual fact, for those who take a human rights approach to this issue, the problem of trafficking and prostitution poses major problems. As the first case from Nepal suggests there have to be strong laws to deal with the horrendous abuse that women and girls are subject to. There must be vigorous law enforcement, and the training and sensitization of the criminal justice system. Walking down Falkland Road, one can feel the presence of organized crime and organized systematic slavery. When governments say they want to take strong action, there is a sense that this is long overdue. The Nepali and Bangladeshi governments have in fact gone overboard with draconian pieces of legislation which give the death penalty to individuals with lower evidentiary standards for their prosecution.[39]

And yet, the situation is far more complicated. The vast majority of women who cross the India Nepali border do so willingly. They have a strong desire to migrate to better their economic and social conditions. This is true about the traffic into Western Europe as well. Their desire to migrate is exploited by traffickers who then bind them over to prostitution. Led by the immigration departments of the western world, there is now a campaign to stop international trafficking. But those of us who have been involved in international negotiations are also clear that it is also a campaign about stopping migration. Women's freedom of travel and movement are being curtailed under strict laws that will prevent women from crossing borders. In Nepal now, women have to get the permission of the men in their families and the village heads to leave their village.[40] Such responses can only be counter productive since many of the women we interviewed often left their homes to escape abuse in the home. In addition if there are strict laws, the law enforcement agencies rarely go against traffickers. In India 80% of the cases filed under "The Prevention of Immoral Traffic Act" are against the women.[41] Strong laws usually result in sex workers being constantly harassed by the law. The force of the Rule of Law will finally rest on the individual sex worker.

---

[39] Ibid., 14.
[40] Ibid., 11.
[41] Ibid., 30.

Can one choose to be a prostitute or a sex worker and should the law respect that choice? This is the question that is at the heart of a great deal of debate. Many feminists claim that the abuses are so horrific that one will have to sacrifice the few who actually make a legitimate choice to do sex work for the protection of the majority. Others argue that sex work has been a constant throughout the years and that sex workers should be treated as workers and endowed with rights. In discussing this, lawyers have to ask a further question, should the law be involved in regulating the sexual practices and choices of individuals? The answer to the dilemma, a way of stopping the abuse with out overly regulating sexual behaviour, may lie in the concept of slavery. The aspects of the first Nepali case that shock the conscience are the facts related to sexual slavery; a person handed over to prostitution under conditions resembling slavery. According to the Foca judgment that has recently been handed down by The International Tribunal of The Former Yugoslavia in a case involving sexual slavery in Bosnia, the Court defined slavery in terms of the exercise of the right of ownership that may include the menace of penalty.[42] The Court also set down some tests and standards on how to determine slavery and slavery like practices. If one uses the prism of slavery as the main anchor, then the State and the law need not get involved in moral debates involving individual choice and preference. Women who are sold into prostitution and experience the horrendous reality of a trafficked life can be the main focus of the campaign against trafficking.

The law's attitudes to sexuality and sexual practices are also relevant for issues of sexual harassment. It has been twenty years since Catherine Mackinnon wrote her book *Sexual Harassment of Working Women: A Case of Sex Discrimination* (1979).[43] Since then, galvanized by her writings and efforts of other women a plethora of statutes have been written around the world that now deal with sexual harassment. In some countries such as The United States, sexual harassment is treated as discrimination in workplaces and educa-

---

[42] See Prosecutor v Dragoljub Kunarac, et. al, case no. IT 96-23-T& IT 96 23/1-T, *International Tribunal For The Former Yugoslavia*, Trial Chamber, February 2001.
[43] Catherine Mackinnon, *Sexual Harassment of Working Women: A Case of Sex Discrimination* (New Haven, CT.: Yale University Press, 1979).

tional institutions.[44] Demands for sexual favours and the existence of hostile working environment may result in lawsuits claiming discrimination in the workplace. In others such as India and Sri Lanka, sexual harassment is a criminal offense carrying a jail sentence.[45] Sexual harassment has always been a problem for working women. In 1988 42% of women working in US federal government offices claimed that they had been victims of sexual harassment.[46] In the US military, two thirds of the women claimed that they had been subject to sexual harassment.[47] Women have put up with this harassment for decades for fear of losing their options, for being seen as troublesome or for "putting up with the boys." Mackinnon and her colleagues changed all that and women throughout the world are safer in schools and educational institutions because of their efforts. Recently, however, civil libertarian Nadine Strossen attacked this feminist legacy from a libertarian perspective. In an article entitled "Defining Sexual Harassment: Sexuality Does Not Equal Sexism"[48] she challenges the whole concept of "a hostile work environment"[49] being a justification for sex discrimination. Under this concept, pornographic pictures, lewd remarks and other forms of sexual speech were seen as offensive, justifying a petitioner's right of compensation. "Hostile Work" environment harassment is defined as "verbal or physical conduct of a sexual nature has the purpose or effect of unreasonably interfering with an individual's job performance or creating, hostile or offensive work environment." Such conduct would be seen as hostile if it appears so to a reasonable person. Citing startling examples such as a university professor having to remove a reproduction of Goya's Nude Maja from his office, she argued that the movement had gone too far. Pointing to another case of a university professor being accused of sexual harassment because she distributed

---

[44] E.E.O.C Regulation to Title VII of the Civil Rights Act of 1964 29 C.F.R. sec. 1604.11 (I 992).

[45] Section 345 of The Sri Lanka Penal Code as amended in 1995.

[46] Beverly Balos and Mary Louise Fellows, *Law and Violence Against Women: Cases and Materials on Systems of Appression,* (Durham NC.: Carolina Academic Press, 1994), 281.

[47] Ibid., 281.

[48] Nadine Strossen, *Defending Pornography: Free Speech, Sex, and the Fight for Women's Rights* (New York: New York University Press, 1995).

[49] Meritor Savings Bank, FSB v Vinson, 477 U.S. 57 19860

pictures of female nudes in an art class, Strossen claimed that the hostile environment clause and sexual harassment strategies generally had chilled free speech and expression in educational institutions and in the workplace. She claimed women were increasingly being seen as cry-babies with no capacity to deal with real life issues. The anti sexual harassment movement, according to Strossen is perverting the relationship between the sexes.

And yet, any woman who has been in a "hostile work environment" knows how debilitating such an environment can be. In such an environment women are usually debased, second-class citizens, always making coffee but never treated as equals. For women, Mackinnon and her colleagues have changed the inter personal dynamics within the workplace forever. Nevertheless Strossen raises an important problem. With regard to any law or regulation that involves behaviour modification, the question remains what are the free speech implications? Mackinnon and Dworkin also led the campaign against pornography and helped draft some strict statutes in certain States in the United States.[50] Again there is an attempt to use the law to define and punish certain types of sexual behaviour.

If one takes the larger picture with regard to women and sexuality, one develops a very contradictory picture. On the one hand, in certain societies, women's rights activists are attempting to secure women's sexual freedom. Fighting against female circumcision, challenging dress codes, and celebrating women's bodies, many activists want to assert women's sexual agency. These developments are linked to the international movement to secure women's reproductive rights as an essential aspect of their human rights. This movement reached its climax in Cairo at the International Conference on Population and Development. Though the drafters did not accept the concept of sexual rights they did say "Reproductive Health, therefore, implies that people are able to have a safe and satisfying sex life and that they have the capability to reproduce and the freedom to decide, if when and how often to do so.[51]

However, at the same time, there is another strand to women's rights activism and that is to use the criminal law to control

---

[50] See the Minneapolis Ordinance regulating pornography, December 30th 1983 amending Minneapolis Code of Ordinance Title vii, chs. 139 & 141.

and punish certain kinds of sexual behavior. Whether with regard to prostitution, sexual conduct in the workplace or pornography, these activists argue that there is no room for abuse. For them sexuality should be strictly controlled, contained and modified so that women will be able to live in dignity and respect.

This tension between sexual freedom and sexual containment has challenged younger writers to formulate new positions. In recent times, along with criticisms of the feminist position on privacy has come a critique of feminist positions that attempt to use the law to regulate sexual behaviour. There is a belief that the law is ill suited for this kind of process and that important issues of freedom of expression are involved. Recognizing that the law must prevent slavery, violence and coercion, there is a belief that speech and "behavioral practices should be changed by other means and not through the law. Gayle Rubin suggests what the law needs is an approach that recognizes pluralistic sexual ethics.[52] Such an approach accepts a variation in sexual expression while ensuring that any expression that is abusive, coercive or violent be punished. The more I work on violence against women, the more I agree that the laws should provide a safety net with regard to certain kinds of practices that are violent, abusive and slavery like whether or not it involves sexuality. But beyond that, attitudes and approaches to sexuality are so diverse and so severely contested that the law should refrain from being intrusive or passing judgment. The boundaries and attitudes of The Rule of Law construct greatly affect the way women perceive and use the law and the legal system. In addition, in subtle ways, the Rule of Law construct conditions our behaviour and our assumptions whether it be about privacy or sexuality. There is another way in which The Rule of Law construct has a profound effect on women. The type of human personality celebrated by the Rule of Law construct, the ideal type of the Enlightenment man, is seen by many as an embodiment of masculine virtues. Kantian in inspiration, this man is endowed with reason and human agency. He makes rational choices in the course of everyday and as an individual faces the consequences of his

[51] See Chap.VII, Para. 7.2, Programme of Action, ICPD, 1994.
[52] Gayle S. Rubin, "Thinking Sex:-Notes for a Radical Theory of the Politics of Sexuality," in Carol Vance (ed.) *Pleasure and Danger: Exploring Female Sexuality*, (London: Routledge & Kegan Paul, 1984), 30.

action. The formulation of "rights" as the basis of legal entitlement focuses on the individual and his rationally determined acts. He, the individual, is the centre of the legal frame not God or the community.[53]

A central tenet of this enlightenment ideal is the ability of individuals to make choices with the resulting imperative to institutions of society to create the conditions so that these choices can be freely made. For women, the right to choose has a particular history. Linked to the struggle for abortion rights, it has been used as the slogan to allow women the right to choose the destiny of their own bodies even at the expense of the life of the fetus. The right to choose has been the linchpin of the reproductive rights movement and movements related to sexual orientation. Women have always argued that the women's movement is about giving women choices of what they want to do with their lives. However, the question is never that simple. What does one do about a woman who ostensibly chooses to commit *Sati* or widow immolation on her husband's pyre? What does one do about a Muslim woman in France who wants to wear a veil to school? What does one do about mothers who are central figures in the circumcision of their daughters, or mothers who abort their female fetuses in search of boy children? What do you do about employers who want to give people the choice as to whether they want maternity leave? Can women choose to do sex work? Can women choose to deny themselves rights?

Women activists researching *Sati* or widow immolation in India point to the fact that allowing women choice in those circumstances would be extremely dangerous. *Sati* is an Indian practice whereby the widow commits suicide on her husband's pyre. It is seen as a "religious act akin to that which the Goddess *Sati* did for her husband Shiva. In mythical terms, it is said to be a sign of the widow's love and devotion for her husband. Once a woman commits *Sati* she becomes a Goddess and temple can be endowed in her name. Many authors like Ashis Nandy have argued that *Sati* is about heroic death and involves a heroic ideal. "Voluntary" *Sati* is seen as a very noble and brave act and individual cases of what appear to be volun-

---

[53] To see an interesting discussion of Kantian ideals in the post colonial setting see Gayatri Spivak, *A Critique of Postcolonial Reason*, (Chicago, University of Chicago

tary *Sati* have been recorded. If a woman really loves her husband and wants to commit *Sati*, should the law stop her?[54] Lata Mani after some detailed research comes to the conclusion that if *Sati* was permitted many families would put pressure on their daughters to commit *Sati* and the daughters would find it difficult to resist.[55] This would lead to great many deaths especially among young widows who are seen as burdens on their families. The law prohibiting *Sati*, the law prohibiting choice, allows women to live and not have to negotiate their lives with their in-laws. If *Sati* was permitted in any form, one widow will be told about the role model of the other widow, placing many women in a great dilemma. The denial of choice then ensures that society cannot pressurise young women to engage in the practice. The same argument is used about Chinese foot binding and female circumcision. Denying choice means that mothers have an excuse to spare their daughters while if the law did not exist their daughters would not be seen as unmarriageable. Where allowing choice means that the structures of power in the society would weigh so down so heavily on individual women that choice would be meaningless, it becomes important to consider denying the possibility of that choice by legislation.

Choice, an important element of the enlightenment ideal. then poses major dilemmas for women. In dealing with these questions are there situations which present us with a clear necessity for denying women choice? As the women's rights campaign is about enhancing choices, it is difficult to single out areas where choice should be limited. However, when it comes to practices like *Sati*, foot binding or female circumcision, the torture standard of "severe pain and suffering" may give us some guidance. The prohibition against torture is generally recognised as *jus cogens*, a principle of 56 international law that cannot be derogated from.[56] Torture in its defini-

---

Press 2000), 31.

[54] Ashis Nandy "*Sati* in Kali Yuga: The Public Debate on Roop Kanwar's Death" in Ashis Nandy, *The Savage Freud*, (Delhi: Oxford University Press, 1995).

[55] See Lata Mani, *Contentious Tradition: The Debate on Sati in Colonial India* (Berkeley, CA.: University of California Press, 1998).

[56] See for example, American Law Institute, *Restatement of The Law Third: The Foreign Relations Law of The United States* (vol 2) sec. 702 at 161. Also see Ian Brownlie, *Principles of Public International Law*, (Oxford: Oxford University Press, 1990), 512-525.

tion under the Torture Convention[57] does require the consent or acquiescence of a public official but many feminists have tried to use the parallel of torture in other areas. Certain practices are torture like and given the international prohibitions relating to inflicting "severe pain and suffering," women may be denied the choice to inflict that pain on themselves or their children. Other cases, not involving severe pain and suffering are far more difficult to judge. Should we support the drive to make maternity leave an issue of choice? If one were a professional woman this seems a natural demand But if one were a factory worker, can one bargain for maternity leave on a equal footing? What about the mother's choice to abort her fetus? In India the vast majority of fetuses aborted since the discovery of sex selection technology have been female. Should the State stop giving information to women about their bodies in the greater interest of saving the life of the female fetus? Should women be given the freedom to do sex work, even when we know that such sex work is run by organized crime? A woman's choice has been a key element in women's emancipation. One could argue that it was part of the struggle to make the enlightenment ideal a common one for men and women. Women, too, would be free, rational and exercising choice. And yet, in some areas the issue of choice poses great dilemmas for women's activists as well as the law. The dilemma of choice is not the only one posed by the enlightenment ideal that is at the root of The Rule of Law, construct. In the 1980s, Carol Gilligan put forward one of the far-reaching critiques of this ideal from a feminist perspective in her book, *In a Different Voice.*[58] After having conducted research with children of different ages, she came to the conclusion that boys and girls are socialised differently. Her research pointed to the fact that the enlightenment ideal is about the way men are socialised and the structures of justice based on this ideal formulate and implement justice in the masculine way. She argues from a young age, women approach the world differently and many of the laws and processes we have in place are deeply alienating to their lived experience.

---

[57] Convention Against Torture and Other Cruel, Inhuman or Degrading Treatment or Punishment adopted 1984, entry into force, 1987.
[58] Carol Gilligan, *In a Different Voice, Psychological Theory and Women's Development*, (Cambridge, MA.: Harvard University Press, 1982).

The Rule of Law construct as outlined in the Anglo-American world and carried to the colonies through the British empire, rests on an adversarial notion of justice. Litigants before a court of law argue adversarialy but with the understanding that winner takes all. According to Gilligan, women and young girls do not see justice through that kind of lens.[59] The young girls she interviewed were far happier trying to find the middle ground, to talk it out and to negotiate a solution. She also argued that young girls were not transfixed by the notion that there were objective principles that applied to everyone requiring obedience and compliance. They were more subjective in their discussion placing primary emphasis on actual lived experience and interpersonal experiences. And finally, young girls were not so emphatic about the primacy of reason. Emotions were important part of their decision making and there seemed to be an alternative ethic revolving around notions of nurture and care that seemed to resonate more with their beliefs.

It is now nearly two decades since Gilligan wrote her book but a great deal of what she has said has become an important part of modern legal understanding. Though initially deeply contested because it appeared to underscore fault lines that separate men from women, the so-called "feminine" perceptions of justice have made their appearance in innovative new experiments. One such experiment is the concept of "Truth Commissions" set up after a terrible violent conflict or a turbulent era. These Commissions like *The South African Truth and Rehabilitation Commission* are not only concerned with adversarial justice. They operate on concepts relating to healing, the importance of the subjective narrative and notions of care and forgiveness.[60] These Commissions have come under some criticism for their lack of emphasis on punishment and accountability of perpetrators but they are innovative ways of dealing with other aspects of pain and suffering that result from injustice and war. Another similar movement is the restorative justice movement in the

---

[59] "The story of Amy and Jake," Carol Gilligan, *op. cit.*, 24-64.

[60] For an interesting account see Martha Minow, *Between Vengeance and Forgiveness: Facing History after Genocide and Mass Violence*, (Boston: Beacon Press, 1998).

United States, especially in the State of Minnesota.[61] Under this movement there is a project in the prisons for the victims of crimes or relatives of the victims to meet the perpetrator on a regular basis, under the supervision of a trained psychologist, to work out issues of pain and accountability on a face to face basis. According to prison officials in Minnesota this is a very important programme and may help prevent the emergence of recurrent criminals who end up seemingly addicted to the criminal justice system.. It can be said that in the beginning of the twentieth century, the Rule of Law construct is being feminised and transformed with greater understanding of the needs of all human beings. The difference between Dicey and Foucault is that Dicey sees The Rule of Law as an essential, ahistorical ideal that is universal, transcending epochs and the moment. For Foucault, The Rule of Law, like any other construct, is a product of its history and like history it never stops. It grows and evolves as power relations and ideas change and transform. Like all concepts it is a dynamic one. As these concepts begin to be globalised, begin to interact with every society and civilisation, they will transform and develop. They will be enriched by the diversity and the history of those civilisations and they will enrich the western world with new frontiers for jurisprudence and legal philosophy. In Sierra Leone, The United Nations called a national conference on The Rule of Law to find out what people felt about this concept.[62] Grassroots organisations as well as policymakers were invited. There was general agreement about representative democracy and the independent judiciary but the women went further. Why they asked does the Rule of law have nothing to say about economic and social rights or the right to survival? As we see the developments from the world around us from Seattle onwards, it appears that this may be a worldwide concern. Perhaps this will point to new directions for the future. In conclusion may I say that when I took up the post of The United Nations Special Rapporteur on Violence Against Women, I thought I had a limited job of evaluating countries based on international standards of

---

[61] *Report of The United Nations Special Rapporteur on Violence Against Women*, (Mission to the United States of America, United Nations Human Rights Commission), E/CN.4/1999/68/ Add.2 (1999)
[62] Oral conversation with the officer of The Office Of The High Commissioner for Human Rights in Sierra Leone in charge of The Rule of Law project.

human rights and women's rights. However, after many years in this job and having gone to many societies, I find that studying these issues has opened up new dimensions, often challenging my assumptions and disturbing my perceptions. Research into women's rights often comes up against deeply held beliefs and highly contested ideas. In the end one finds more questions than answers. My only hope is that in some sense by highlighting the issues I can take the legacy of feminism forward, a legacy that one young feminist described in a very fitting way She said the feminist legacy is "one of misbehaving: by speaking radical truths to power, by speaking the unspeakable."[63]

Radhika Coomaraswamy *directs the International Centre for Ethnic Studies, Colombo and chairs Sri Lanka's Human Rights Commission. She served as the United Nations' Special Rapporteur on Violence Against Women for a decade.*

---

[63] Morris, *op. cit.*, 348.

www.ingramcontent.com/pod-product-compliance
Lightning Source LLC
Chambersburg PA
CBHW031210270326
41931CB00006B/507